Bishop George Berkeley

Three Dialogues
between
Hylas and Philonous

edited, with an introduction by

David Hilbert & John Perry

Areté Press

We would like to thank:

The students of the Soto House Seminars on Berkeley, for allowing us to try our idea out on them;

Katie Hilbert, Frenchie Perry, Sue Perry and Ron Rubin for encouragement at every step of the way;

James Woodward and Alan Donagan for helpful comments on the introduction;

and Barbara DiPalma for her careful proofreading and advice.

David Hilbert and John Perry

Table of Contents

INTRODUCTION

1. Why Study the Dialogues?

Bishop George Berkeley of Cloyne believed that reality consists entirely of minds and their ideas. In his *Three Dialogues between Hylas and Philonous*, the bishop's spokesman Philonous patiently explains the fundamental tenets of this "immaterialism" to his friend Hylas.

Three Dialogues was Berkeley's second attempt to convince his contemporaries of the virtues of immaterialism; his earlier book, *The Principles of Human Knowledge*, failed miserably in this respect. The *Three Dialogues* was an attempt to present immaterialism in a way that would be more accessible to the general public. It was just as unsuccessful as its predecessor. Neither book was widely read; Berkeley's philosophy was chiefly known as the subject of humorous anecdotes related by people who had never read his work. Berkeley's views struck his contemporaries as too bizarre to take seriously. Surely his ideas are even more unlikely to gain acceptance in today's materialistic world. So of what interest could these dialogues be to a modern student of philosophy?

We think there are several good reasons for such a student to study the *Dialogues*. For one thing, Berkeley is fun to read. He lays out arguments, both good and bad, with great clarity. He states objections to his own views, and answers them candidly. His writings have a lively quality to them that suggests the author must have been an interesting character, and Berkeley lived up to this. Berkeley was not a closeted philosopher, but a man of action who devoted his life to several important missions. Some of these pursuits marked him as a bit of an eccentric — he spent enormous amounts of time and energy promoting the virtues of tar water, for example. But another mission led to a trip to America. This trip had considerable influence on American philosophy and even American higher education, although he never realized his ambition to found a college in the Americas. Indeed, Berkeley's name is probably more prominent in higher education than that of any other philosopher. Berkeley, California, the home of one of the great American universities, is named for him, as are Berkeley College and the Berkeley Fellowships at Yale. Berkeley's only real follower among his contemporaries was an American philosopher named Samuel Johnson, who taught at Yale and was one of the founders and the first president of Columbia University.

A second reason for studying Berkeley is the influence of his ideas. Although he did not convince the contemporaries at whom his works were aimed — men like Jonathan Swift and Bishop Butler — and although he has never had very many disciples, the influence of Berkeley's ideas has been enormous. He helped introduce two new ideas into modern philosophy: phenomenalism and idealism. Phenomenalism is the epistemological thesis that what we learn through perception, and use in action, are simply the connections between actions and experiences; ordinary things are just conceptual devices for organizing this knowledge, not the objects of it. Idealism is the metaphysical thesis that reality consists of minds and their ideas and nothing else. Berkeley put these ideas together; other philosophers have pulled them apart. Either way, they have been two of the enduring themes of philosophy since Berkeley wrote.

Even though few of Berkeley's contemporaries agreed with his conclusions, his work provides a valuable window for looking at the eighteenth century. The strikingly different view he advocated betrays not so much a different starting point from that of his contemporaries, as a more determined examination of the path to which those assumptions can lead than most of them were willing to undertake. Because the problem he dealt with is one we can grasp but his way of looking at it is so different from ours, we can learn a great deal from studying Berkeley about the eighteenth century way of looking at things.

But the most important reason for the modern philosophy student to study Berkeley is that he is a good philosopher. There is no better introduction to the basic philosophical problems about perception and knowledge than wrestling with his doctrines and arguments. The fact that the modern student is likely to resist becoming an immaterialist is really an educational advantage. As Hume wrote, Berkeley "produces no conviction, but admits of no refutation." Dealing with a philosopher who challenges our basic way of looking at things and who does so through argument and analysis and defense of an alternative vision can be the most rewarding philosophical education of all. Berkeley is such a philosopher.

2. Perception, Action, and the World

In this introduction, we first focus on what we feel was Berkeley's greatest contribution, the explanation of the informativeness of experience that underlies his phenomenalism. Then we consider the most significant problem he faced in developing his insights: what to do about ordinary objects. There are many other issues to explore in Berkeley's philosophy, as a glance at the list of suggested readings will verify.

2.1 Ideas vs Things

Experience is informative: it gives us the information that we need to act intelligently in the world. Suppose, for example, that I am hungry.[1] What is it reasonable for me to do? It all depends. If there is an apple in front of me, reaching out and grabbing it might be a good idea. If not, perhaps a walk to the kitchen will help. In deciding what to do, I need to use what I know about the world around me. And the information I have about the world around me I get from experience. We can imagine terrifying situations, in which we have no way of getting the information we need to act intelligently. And some of us have been in such situations on occasion. But most of the time, we seem to have the ability to find out what we need to know, in order to figure out what to do. This principle, that experience provides us with the information we need for successful action, we call *the principle of informative experience*.

Common sense supplies us with a straightforward account of how this works. Central to this account is the category of objects that we will call *ordinary things*. Examples of ordinary things are apples, tables, chairs, refrigerators, and the like. We are able to perceive ordinary things. We assume that they often continue to exist even when they are not perceived and that, even when they are perceived, they have more properties than the perceiver can detect all at once. For example, I do not perceive the taste of the apple when it is on the table across the room. When I pick it up and bite into it, I do taste it. According to common sense the success of our action depends on these ordinary things. Because there is an apple in front of me, my coordinated movement of arm, lips, jaws, and throat is successful in relieving my hunger. Thus common sense provides a

---

[1] The authors will pretend to be one person when it is convenient to have examples which use the first person singular.

justification of the principle of informative experience that relies on two key components:

(1)   the success of our actions depends on the properties and relations of ordinary things

(2)   perception gives us knowledge of the properties and relations of ordinary things.

In spite of the clarity and simplicity of this justification of the principle of informative experience, philosophers since antiquity have been suspicious of it. In particular the truth of (2) has been repeatedly questioned. The intellectual world focused on these doubts when they received a new formulation in the seventeenth and eighteenth centuries with the rise of the "New Philosophy." This term was introduced by Pierre Bayle in his *Dictionary* of 1697. Bayle thought that he had identified a number of assumptions shared by Descartes, Malebranche, and other important philosophers and scientists. Bayle also thought these shared assumptions led to the conclusion that perceptual knowledge is impossible.[2] Since Berkeley was in large measure reacting to what he saw as serious problems in the New Philosophy we will sketch some of its doctrines. In particular, we will look at the considerations that led the New Philosophers to reject (2) and at the alternative justification of the principle of informative experience that was needed once (2) had been rejected.

To see the problem with (2), consider the experience I have when looking at an apple. If I close my eyes, the experience ceases — but surely the apple is still there. If I move away from the apple, or look at it from a different angle, the character of my experience changes, but the apple itself remains unchanged. (The fact that my experience of an object can change with changes in position, lighting, and other such conditions while the object itself remains unchanged is called *the relativity of perception*.) And if I were having a dream about an apple, I might have an experience just like the one I have when looking at an apple, but there

---

2   There is some controversy as to whether the various philosophers grouped together by Bayle actually held the views he attributed to them, but it is undeniable that Berkeley was very much influenced by Bayle's description of the philosophical situation of the late seventeenth century.

would be no apple there. One might argue that there is a difference between the apple itself and the aspect of my experience that represents it. It is this latter thing, the aspect of the experience, that ceases to exist when I close my eyes, that changes as I move away from the apple, and that might exist if I were dreaming even if the apple was not there. Considerations like these (which Hylas and Philonous rehearse for us in the *First Dialogue*) led philosophers to draw a distinction between those things we perceive immediately and those we perceive mediately.

A slightly altered version of an example Philonous uses in the *First Dialogue* will help in understanding this distinction. Suppose you read in the newspaper that it is raining in Miami. What you *immediately* perceive is the pattern of letters and words on the page in front of you. From this you *infer* that something is happening in Florida. You might say, "I see that it is raining in Miami." But, strictly speaking, you see the words on the page, and infer, based perhaps on the reliability of the newspaper you are reading, that things are the way it says they are. One way to describe the relation between the words on the page and the weather in Miami is to say that the words represent the weather in Miami. In order to get beyond the representation to what it represents you need to make an inference based on something other than what it is that you immediately see.

The New Philosophers pushed this distinction, between the immediate and mediate objects of perception, one step further. The facts of the relativity of perception, like the changing perceived size of the apple discussed above, led to the claim that what is *immediately* perceived is not even the pattern of marks on the paper, but certain images in the mind of the perceiver. It is possible for you to have those images in your mind even if there were no newspaper — say if you were dreaming about reading a newspaper. But in this case you take those images to mean that there are marks on the paper, and you take the marks on the paper to mean that there is rain in Miami. Your knowledge of the weather in Miami is *doubly mediated*. This is *the theory of representative ideas*: that all we are ever immediately aware of are images in our own minds and that these images are representations of things that exist outside of perception. Just as the words in the newspaper are representations of the weather in Miami, the ideas in your mind are representations of the marks on the page that constitute the words. On the theory of representative ideas our knowledge of the world outside our mind is always mediated by our awareness of our own ideas. Moving beyond our ideas always involves inference.

We are never directly aware of anything other than the contents of our own minds.

The theory of representative ideas, as described by Bayle and developed by Locke, has one particularly important advantage over the view we attributed to common sense. It allows us to account for *things going wrong*. That is, it allows us to account for the difference between veridical perception and error. Error occurs when the ideas we immediately perceive do not truly represent how things are. Since the theory has both ideas and things, it can account for error in terms of the failure of ideas to correspond in the right way to things. Principles (1) and (2) do not draw this distinction and consequently do not provide common sense with an account of perceptual error. The New Philosophy neatly solves this difficulty by denying that what we immediately perceive are the things themselves.

This solution to the problem of error, however, comes with a price attached. It involves giving up the claim that the objects that we are immediately aware of in perception are ordinary things. (Berkeley will argue that it ultimately involves the denial that there are ordinary things at all.) It also raises a problem about how we can justify the principle of informative experience. According to the New Philosophers we do not immediately perceive the things that our ideas represent and that determine the success or failure of our actions. Strictly speaking, I never see the apple which my various ideas of red and round and sweet represent.

To complicate the situation, the New Philosophers made the additional claim that things, as opposed to ideas, have no color, taste, or odor. The only properties the apple has itself, according to the New Philosophy, are its spatial qualities and the spatial qualities of its parts. The colorless, tasteless, odorless things of the New Philosophy do not seem much like the ordinary things of common sense. We will follow Berkeley and call them *material things*. In this usage "material thing" is not just a synonym for "ordinary thing." The theory of representative ideas, then, amounts to the claim that all we are ever immediately aware of are ideas which may or may not represent *material* things. These material things are the best candidates the New Philosopher has to offer for the ordinary things of common sense — but the fit is not perfect.

This aspect of the New Philosophy, although disturbing and clearly inconsistent with common sense, is not the main problem faced by the theory of representative ideas. Let us call the principle that our ideas normally represent material things the way they are *the principle of representation*. The New Philosophy needs this principle to explain the informativeness of experience. But what reason do we have for accepting it? Descartes had provided good reasons *not* to accept it.[3] How do we know that we are not just having a consistent dream? How do we know that our perceptions are not just the result of an evil demon manipulating our minds?

Let's return for a moment to the case of the newspaper. We can check the reliability of a newspaper in various ways. I could see if the television news also reports rain in Miami. I could look at other newspapers. And if I live in Miami, I can just look out the window. In this last case, I would be directly testing my indirect source of information (the newspaper). This doesn't work with perception. Perception is my *only* access to the external world. I have no more direct way to check it. I can check one set of perceptions against another. If I think I see an apple, I can reach out and touch it to make sure it is there. But I have no way of checking my whole faculty of perception. Since material things are always inaccessible to perception, we cannot make use of some of our perceptions to check the other parts. Nowhere is there the kind of direct access that it seems we would need to get started on a justification of the principle of representation.

Without the principle of representation the New Philosophy has no way of justifying the principle of informative experience. The New Philosophers held a slightly revised version of (1): the success or failure of our actions are determined by the properties of material things. What we directly know about are our own ideas. Without the principle of representation to connect the two, the New Philosophy leaves us with no basis for action.

2.2 Berkeley's Concern with Skepticism

Berkeley thought the New Philosophers could not avoid these skeptical problems and that they would have disastrous consequences for practical as well as theoretical affairs. He wrote *The Three Dialogues* to rescue us from the paradoxes of philosophy and return us to a belief in the truths of common sense.

---

3. See Descartes, *Meditations on First Philosophy*, especially Meditation I.

Berkeley was sympathetic with much of the New Philosophy. Of Locke, he wrote:

> Wonderful in Locke that he could when advanced in years see at all through a mist that had been so long gathering and was consequently thick. This more to be admired than that he didn't see farther.[4]

In spite of his admiration for Locke, Berkeley could not accept what he saw as the inevitable outcome of accepting the New Philosophers' distinction between those things that really exist and determine the success of action and those things of which we are immediately aware, our perceptions or ideas. Berkeley claims:

> We have been led into very dangerous errors, by supposing a twofold existence of the objects of sense, the one *intelligible*, or in the mind, the other *real* and without the mind. . . . This which. . . is the very root of *skepticism*; for so long as men thought that real things subsisted without the mind, and that their knowledge was only so far forth *real* as it was conformable to *real things*, it follows, they could not be certain that they had any real knowledge at all.[5]

According to Berkeley, the New Philosophy leads directly to the denial that we can know anything about the real things that supposedly lie outside the mind. Berkeley thought, and argues brilliantly in the *First Dialogue*, that the theory of representative ideas leads directly to the conclusion that we cannot have any knowledge of the material things that the New Philosophy tells us are the objects of all practical knowledge. In other words, the New Philosophy's own principles lead to skepticism about the very things it tells us we need to know about.

Just how profound Berkeley's dissatisfaction with the New Philosophy was can be seen from his claim that the philosophical principles that his contemporaries shared lead philosophers to, "spend [their] lives in doubting of those things which other men evidently know, and believing those things which they laugh at, and despise."[6] Berkeley thought the ultimate upshot of the New Philosophy was the complete rejection of

---

4. George Berkeley, *Philosophical Commentaries,* in Luce and Jessop, Vol. 1, p. 71.
5. *Principles,* § 86.
6. Preface, p. 3.

common sense and with it the grounds for successful action, good morals, and belief in God. The mistakes that Berkeley saw in the accepted philosophy of his time were not just idle mistakes in theoretical principles. In his view, they had profound negative consequences in practical, moral, and religious areas as well.

Berkeley believed that providing a philosophical grounding for our common sense beliefs would allow us to move in all areas of life with more secure footing, not just in speculative philosophy. He claims that,

> If the principles, which I here endeavor to propagate, are admitted for true; the consequences which, I think, evidently flow from thence, are, that atheism and skepticism will be utterly destroyed, many intricate points made plain, great difficulties solved, several useless parts of science retrenched, speculation referred to practice, and men reduced from paradoxes to common sense.[7]

Thus the goal of the *Three Dialogues* is to provide a solution to the problem of skepticism, to provide a secure foundation for our ordinary beliefs about the world, and in particular to defend the reliability of the senses.

2.3 The Move to Phenomenalism

The New Philosophy depended on the principle of representation to connect what we can know with what we need to know in order to act successfully. Berkeley thought that the principle of representation was indefensible. Part of his reason for thinking this was, as we will see later, that he thought incoherent the New Philosophers' claim that there are real things that are unperceivable. Berkeley did, however, accept the claim of the New Philosophers that all we are immediately aware of is our own experience. This conjunction of views would seem to leave Berkeley in an uncomfortable position. He accepts the arguments that lead to the theory of representative perception and argues further that this theory leads inevitably to skepticism regarding the possibility of practical knowledge. Still, in spite of this, he makes the claim, as we have seen, that he has refuted skepticism.

Berkeley had a radical insight that he thought would allow him to defend himself against the objection that this position is inconsistent. As

---

7. *Ibid.*, p. 4.

he puts it in the last sentence of the *Three Dialogues*, "the same principles which at first view lead to *skepticism*, pursued to a certain point, bring men back to common sense."[8]

To understand Berkeley's bold solution to the skeptical problems posed by the New Philosophy, we need to return to our original problem, the justification of the principle of informative experience. The common sense justification of the principle of informative experience was based on two principles: (1) the success of our actions depends on the properties and relations of ordinary things and (2) perception gives us knowledge of the properties and relations of ordinary things. The New Philosophers modified this account. Instead of our original two principles, we now have three somewhat different principles:

(1') The success of our actions depend on the properties and relations of material things.

(2') Perception directly gives us knowledge only of the character of our own experience.

(PR) Our experience normally represents material things as having the properties and relations that they actually have.

Without the principle of representation (PR), the New Philosophy has no way of explaining how our experience can guide action. If one accepts, as Berkeley did, the move from (2) to (2') but rejects (PR), it seems that one has no way to justify the principle of informative experience. The only things we *can* know about are the properties of our ideas but what we *need* to know are the properties of material things. It is in this sense that Berkeley thinks the New Philosophy leads to skepticism. Berkeley suggests a radical solution to this problem: give up (1') as well as (PR) and construct an entirely different justification for the principle of informative experience.

To understand Berkeley's solution, we need to introduce the notion of an "action-experience connection." Let's return to the case of the apple.

---

8. *Third Dialogue*, p. 93.

Now let's look very closely at the facts, trying not to interpret them through the earlier justifications of the principle of informative experience. Basically, they are as follows. There are a number of different situations I might be in. In some of them, a certain action — the coordinated movement of arm, hand, lips, tongue, jaw, and throat — will lead me to experience relief from hunger. In other situations, the very same action will lead to other experiences. What I need to know, in the most basic terms, is which of those situations I am in. That is, I need to know what the prevailing action-experience connections are — which actions will lead to which experiences. This is what I need to know, *and it is all that I need to know*. Nothing else matters.

Moreover, says Berkeley, this is just what perception tells us. When I see the apple, what do I learn? I learn how my actions will affect my experiences. Making a certain movement will result in the relief of hunger. If I had seen a billiard ball instead, what would I have learned? I would have learned that the same movement would lead to a nasty experience, that involved in breaking a tooth, rather than to the relief of hunger. If I saw nothing there, I would have learned that the movement would just be an empty pawing in the air. *The role of perception is not to tell us what material things are like, but merely to tell us what the prevailing connections between action and experience are.*

We will use the term *phenomenalism* for the view that all we can know, and all we need to know, are action-experience connections. Berkeley replaces the earlier justification of the principle of informative experience with a new and radically different one. This justification makes use of two new principles:

(1") The success of our actions depends on the prevailing action-experience connections.

(2") Perception gives us knowledge of the prevailing action-experience connections — the objects we directly perceive are signs of what we will experience if we perform various actions.

In this way, Berkeley thought that he could explain how we can know what we need to know in order to act successfully. Although we cannot know anything about the unperceivable material things of the New

Philosophers, perception reveals to us which action-experience connections prevail at any given time.

Principle (2") may seem dubious on Berkeley's view. There is still a gap between what we directly perceive and what we need to know, just as there is in the New Philosophy. To see this, think of having an experience of a new kind — say, the first time you saw a billiard ball. Billiard balls are unusually heavy objects for their size, and the first time you saw one you may have been surprised by the feeling of heft you got when you picked it up. The next time you saw one, you expected this feeling of heft. So you came to associate a certain action-experience connection with the billiard ball perception. But then it seems that there is inference here, and a gap between immediate and mediate perception.

Berkeley can reply there is a big difference between the two theories. On each theory, we come to believe something that goes beyond what is immediately perceived. According to the theory of representative ideas, we come to believe in a material object, the existence of which we can never directly check. On Berkeley's theory we come to believe that, if we perform certain actions, we will have certain experiences. This belief can be checked just by taking the appropriate action. The dispute is over what the ideas we have in perception *mean*. Berkeley can give an account of how we can learn the meaning of our ideas and how we can check as to their accuracy. But the theorist of representative ideas cannot provide such an account.

On Berkeley's theory, the meaning of our ideas is like the meaning of the patterns of ink in the newspaper. There is inference involved, but it is one we can check. We learn to associate certain experience-action connections with certain types of perceptions through experience; we can check the accuracy of any particular idea, so interpreted, through experience. It is through discerning regularities in our experience, constant associations between different kinds of experience and constant associations between actions and experiences, that we discover the action-experience connections we need to know. Berkeley calls these regularities within experience "laws of nature" and makes the point that it is laws of nature that underwrite our knowledge of action-experience connections. As he puts in it in *The Principles*,

> That food nourishes, sleep refreshes, and fire warms us; that to sow in the seed-time is the way to reap in the harvest, and, in general, that

to obtain such or such ends, such or such means are conducive, all this we know... only by the observation of the settled laws of Nature, without which we should be all in uncertainty and confusion, and a grown man no more know how to manage himself in the affairs of life, than an infant just born.[9]

Berkeley's position depends on a belief in the reliability of induction. What we have experienced in the past is a good guide to what we will experience in the future. It is possible to be skeptical on this point too, as Hume was later to point out. All our experience can guarantee is what things have been like. It cannot establish what they will be like without appeal to the principle of the uniformity of nature. There is nothing in Berkeley's philosophy that provides a satisfying answer to these Humean problems.

But Berkeley does provide a solution to the skeptical problem that bothered him — the problem that on the New Philosophy our expectations about the future have to be based on beliefs about things we have never experienced at all. On Berkeley's theory, the justification of such expectations depends on the principle of representation — a principle of which we have not, and could not, perceive a single confirming instance. Thus Berkeley's phenomenalism allows him to escape the skeptical dilemma that is posed by the New Philosophy and to put useful knowledge of the world on an entirely new footing.

2.4 Phenomenalism and Common Sense

Berkeley's phenomenalism, although it solves his skeptical problem, leaves him with another. The material things of the New Philosophy are out of the picture. Nothing that is not an element of experience plays any role in Berkeley's explanation of action and knowledge. According to Berkeley, not only are material things useless, but the very concept of an object that exists without being perceived is incoherent. He adopted the slogan *esse est percipi,* to be is to be perceived. This emphasizes that there is no role in his philosophy for anything but minds and ideas. But in rejecting the existence of anything beyond our ideas, it seems as if Berkeley has also rejected the ordinary things of common sense. Apples, tables, chairs, and all such familiar objects have no role to play in his

---

9. *Principles,* § 31.

explanation of the possibility of successful action. So, it seems that Berkeley has solved the problem of skepticism at the expense of common sense.

Berkeley could have said "So much the worse for common sense." As we have seen, the New Philosophers were perfectly happy to deviate from common sense when it conflicted with their philosophical principles. Berkeley, however, was not this kind of philosopher. One of the sources of his dissatisfaction with the New Philosophy was its deviation from common sense. Berkeley tried to rescue as much of common sense as he could within the constraints of his phenomenalism. This led him to claim that ordinary things just are ideas, or collections of ideas. In this way, Berkeley attempted to rescue the ordinary things of common sense by identifying them with the experiences that matter according to the phenomenalist explanation of action.

Before evaluating this project, we should pause to appreciate the boldness of Berkeley's project. He accepts principles that he admits lead to skepticism. Then, by a radical regrounding of our knowledge, he attempts both to dissolve the skeptical problem and to show that what we know according to this theory are just the things we always thought we knew. With his identification of ideas and things, Berkeley thinks that he has revealed how his principles can help us to act sensibly in a world composed of apples and billiard balls, tables and chairs. As Berkeley has Philonous claim near the end of the *Dialogues*,

> I do not pretend to be a setter-up of *new notions*. My endeavors tend only to unite and place in a clearer light that truth, which was before shared between the vulgar and the philosophers: the former being of opinion, that *those things they immediately perceive are the real things;* and the latter, that *the things immediately perceived, are ideas which exist only in the mind.* Which two notions put together, do in effect constitute the substance of what I advance.[10]

Berkeley claims that to be is to be perceived and that no ordinary person ever thought differently. As we will see, he cannot consistently maintain his identification of ideas with things, although he can come much closer than most of his contemporaries thought. He is often accused of having

---

10. *Third Dialogue*, pp. 92-93.

denied the existence ordinary things, and there is some justice to this accusation. But what the reader of Berkeley's philosophy should keep in mind is that Berkeley himself did not believe that this was true.

3. Berkeley's Alternatives

We have seen that Berkeley's great epistemological and metaphysical vision leaves him with a serious problem. Where do ordinary objects, such as tables and chairs and trees fit into his system? Before addressing the question of what Berkeley *did* think, we want to look at four different things he has *been taken* to have thought.

3.1 Discontinuous Realism

Ronald Knox wrote a famous limerick, which captures a popular view of Berkeley:

> There once was a man who said "God,
> Must find it exceedingly odd,
> That this sycamore tree
> Continues to Be
> When there's no one about in the Quad."

On this view, the objects Berkeley has in mind when he says "to be is to be perceived" are ordinary objects, like sycamore trees, and the perceivers he has in mind are human beings. This raises an obvious problem, which occurs to almost every student who reads Berkeley's *Dialogues*: What keeps these things in existence when we are not there to perceive them? Students are often reminded of the light inside the refrigerator. Does it go off when one closes the door? One can never tell, because once the door is closed, one cannot see whether the light is off. Similarly, it might seem that one could never check Berkeley's view. No matter how quickly one turns around to check whether the objects behind one have disappeared, it won't be quick enough. One can never show Berkeley wrong by perceiving an unperceived object. This suggests a response Berkeley might have had to the problem: "For all anyone can know, things do pop in and out of existence depending on whether someone is perceiving them. How could anyone ever perceive anything that would prove me wrong about that?" But although no one may have been able to *prove* that Berkeley was wrong on this point, Berkeley wasn't really a *discontinuous realist*. The spirit of Berkeley's solution to this problem is expressed in the following reply to Knox's limerick by an anonymous scholar:

> Dear Sir: Your astonishment's odd;
> I am always about in the Quad;
> So the Sycamore tree
> Will continue to be,
> As observed by yours faithfully, God.

This brings us to our next interpretation of Berkeley's view, *continuous realism*.

3.2 Continuous Realism
As the reply to Knox's limerick hints, Berkeley tried to use the continuous existence of things to prove the existence of God:

> When I deny sensible things an existence out of the mind, I do not mean my mind in particular, but all minds. Now it is plain they have an existence exterior to my mind, since I find them by experience to be independent of it. There is therefore some other mind wherein they exist, during the intervals between the times of my perceiving them.... And as the same is true, with regard to all other finite created spirits; it necessarily follows, there is an *omnipresent eternal Mind*, which knows and comprehends all things, and exhibits them to our view in such a manner, and according to such rules as he himself has ordained, and are by us termed the *Laws of Nature*.[11]

This passage calls on God to play two rather different roles. The first role is that envisioned in the response to Knox's limerick: God perceives things in the intervals when no human (or other "finite spirit") is perceiving them (or, at any rate, knowing or comprehending them), thus keeping them in existence.[12] The second role played by God in Berkeley's philoso-

---

11. *Third Dialogue*, p. 63.
12. If comprehending or knowing are not kinds of perceiving, there is a problem here for Berkeley's thesis that to be is to be perceived.

phy is that of producing ideas in us according to certain rules that he himself has ordained.

The second role is clearly crucial for Berkeley: it is God's fixed intentions to produce ideas in us in a regular way that makes experience informative. It is the first role, however, that allows Berkeley to offer an account of the ordinary things of common sense. Ordinary things like sycamore trees are perceived by a number of minds, including God's. For such ordinary things, to be is to be perceived; God's perception keeps them continuously in existence. Of our four interpretations, this view, continuous realism, allows Berkeley to come closest to the common-sense that he saw threatened by the New Philosophy and that he hoped to save.

Although continuous realism provides a natural account of how ordinary things could fit into Berkeley's immaterialism, it suffers from serious problems. It is subject to the same sort of problem in accounting for perceptual error that we saw earlier with naive realism. And, in addition, it is inconsistent with Berkeley's own attempts to account for the possibility of perceptual error. Continuous realism identifies ordinary things with ideas or collections of ideas. But ideas, being immediately perceived, are just as they are perceived to be. This is a key tenet about which Berkeley and the New Philosophers agreed. There is no possibility of misperceiving the ideas presently before the mind. As Berkeley puts it in discussing a case of apparent misperception, a person's mistake in a case of misperception "lies not in what he perceives immediately and at present (it being a manifest contradiction to suppose he should err in respect of that)."[13] So, if ordinary things were ideas or collections of ideas (as Berkeley claimed), they must be just as they are perceived to be. According to continuous realism, it is not possible to misperceive an ordinary thing.

Just as the claims attributed to naive realism earlier lead to serious difficulty, the denial of the possibility of misperceiving ordinary things leads to problems for continuous realism. An example of Berkeley's will help to make clear the source of the difficulty.

> *Phil.* Suppose now one of your hands hot, and the other cold, and that they are both at once put into the same vessel of water, in an

---

13. *Third Dialogue,* p. 71.

intermediate state; will not the water seem cold to one hand, and warm to the other?

Hyl. It will.

Phil. Ought we not therefore by your principles to conclude, it is really both cold and warm at the same time, that is, according to your own concession, to believe an absurdity.[14]

Continuous realism with its denial of the possibility of misperception cannot avoid the conclusion that one and the same thing is both hot and cold. As Philonous points out, however, no ordinary thing can be both hot and cold at the same time.

What we want to say about these kinds of cases is that one or both of the perceptions is in error: there is a difference between the way the thing is and the way it appears to be. We need this distinction because, as examples of this kind show, the qualities that we perceive things to have depend not just on the qualities those things have but also on other qualities as well including properties of the person doing the perceiving. But continuous realism does not seem to have the resources to make this distinction. As an account of perceptual knowledge, continuous realism founders on the problem of error.[15]

Yet, as an interpretation of Berkeley, continuous realism has a great deal of plausibility. The limerick captures one real strain in Berkeley's thought, a strain that has been picked up by a number of readers of Berkeley's work. Although continuous realism is not entailed by the passage regarding God's role in sustaining the existence of things, it is the most natural interpretation. However, when Berkeley turned his attention to the problem of perceptual error he was led in quite a different direction, as we will we see in the next section.

3.3 Unsupported Phenomenalism

If the *esse-est-percipi* principle does not apply to ordinary things, to what does it apply? When we look at Berkeley's own words, the answer seems clear: the principle applies to *sensible objects*. But what are sensible objects?

---

14. *First Dialogue*, p. 13-14.
15. Continuous realism also suffers from problems regarding the possibility of sharing ideas with God. For a discussion of this problem, see Furlong, E. J., "Berkeley and the tree in the quad," in Martin and Armstrong.

The two realist interpretations of Berkeley take sensible objects to be ordinary objects. The difference between the two interpretations is simply on the issue of whether ordinary objects have a continuous or an interrupted existence. But if one takes sensible objects to be the *qualities* of ordinary objects, one arrives at a very different picture of Berkeley's philosophy.

By "qualities," we mean such things as the redness of the apple in front of me, or the solidity I feel when I touch the keys on the keyboard. On this interpretation, it is only the qualities of objects whose existence is constituted by, and hence guaranteed by, perception. It is not ordinary things that are ideas, but the sensible qualities of ordinary things.

This interpretation, which fits much better with Berkeley's phenomenalism, is motivated by his discussion of perceptual error. Hylas poses the problem of perceptual error to Philonous using the example of an oar partially immersed in water. The oar looks, as things half in and half out of water typically do, as if it were bent. In Berkeley's discussion of this objection we see him make the move from things to qualities. Philonous says, of the person fooled by the oar's appearance,

> He is not mistaken with regard to the ideas he actually perceives; but in the inferences he makes from his present perceptions. Thus in the case of the oar, what he immediately perceives by sight is certainly crooked; and so far he is in the right. But if he thence conclude, that upon taking the oar out of the water he shall perceive the same crookedness; or that it would effect his touch, as crooked things are wont to do; in that he is mistaken.[16]

Let's look closely at these remarks. What does Berkeley mean when he says, ". . . in the case of the oar, what he immediately perceives by sight is certainly crooked; and so far he is in the right." Does he mean that the *oar* is crooked? This would fly in the face of common sense. A bit later, his meaning becomes clear. What is perceived is not a crooked oar, but "crookedness." The person in the boat immediately perceives the crookedness and expects to continue seeing crookedness when the oar is removed from the water.

---

16. *Third Dialogue*, p. 70.

What has happened to the oar itself in this discussion? It is not what is immediately perceived. Does it then become, as in the New Theory, something inferred? Berkeley wouldn't want to put it that way. What is inferred from the experience of crookedness is that a certain action-experience connection prevails. It is inferred that the action of pulling the oar out of the water will lead to a continued experience of crookedness. One movement of inference is from one kind of experience to another, not from experience to something beyond experience.

Berkeley thus moves to a position in which ordinary things are neither identified with ideas nor taken to be objects beyond the ideas. In Berkeley's system, ordinary things really have no place at all. Common sense is defended only by paraphrasing our language about ordinary things in terms of talk about ideas. Berkeley seems to be taking the view here that he expressed in a different context, namely, "That in such things we ought to think with the learned, and speak with the vulgar."[17]

On this view, the basic facts that we know about, form expectations about, and act on the basis of, are ideas — subjective sensations and memories of colors, sounds, and the like. What common sense calls "making a mistake about the shape of an oar" turns out to be a matter of inference. The inference is not one from the nature of ideas to the nature of some unperceived thing causing those ideas, but rather from a perception of one idea to an expectation of another idea. The mistake consists of what seemed earlier to be its consequences — the expectations about the sensations of touch and sight that one would have under altered circumstances, if one felt the oar or looked at it after raising it from the water.

On this interpretation, ordinary objects like oars and trees are just devices for organizing our experiences. But now we face a question similar to the one we raised above, when we considered Berkeley as a realist. *Whose* experiences? If we are just talking about the experiences of finite minds like ourselves, Berkeley's world has shrunk even further than the one Knox objected to in his famous limerick. The tree isn't there, even when someone *is* about in the Quad. All that exists are that person's experiences of qualities of the sort that trees have.

Is that really all there is? Is such a denuded world the price we have to pay to evade skepticism? As Andrew Baxter, one of Berkeley's eighteenth-century critics wrote, "This is, I think, as if one should advance,

---

17. *Principles*, § 51.

that the best way for a woman to silence those who may attack her reputation, is to turn a common prostitute. He puts us into a way of denying all things, that we may get rid of the absurdity of those who deny some things."[18]

We might imagine Berkeley biting the bullet. What possible experience could prove this theory wrong? After all, who has ever experienced anything beyond the qualities of the objects he or she perceives? And who has ever experienced one of these qualities when no one was perceiving it?

Some later empiricists (such as Hume, Mill, and James) at least toyed with biting this particular bullet. But not Berkeley. For him, a world consisting of fleeting, distinct, and unconnected existences would make no sense at all.

It is important to realize that, for Berkeley, ideas are completely passive. No idea causes any other idea. Believing that all there is to reality consists of ideas and perceiving subjects, Berkeley therefore does not think that there is any causation except among perceivers. That is to say, as Berkeley admitted in his earlier book *The Principles of Human Knowledge*, it is not the case that fire heats or water cools or in general that any causal statements of this type are true. All that is true is that perceptions of fire are generally associated with perceptions of greater heat and that perceptions of water are associated with ideas of greater coolness.

Unsupported phenomenalism, then, would leave Berkeley with no answer at all to the question of *why* we perceive one thing — have one experience — rather than another. *Why* does one set of action-experience connections prevail rather than another? *Why*, when I reach out, on the occasion of having the experience of "seeing an apple," do I find, when I reach out, that I have the experience of "touching an apple"? We can't appeal to the apple: it's just a device for keeping track of these connections, not an explanation of them. We can't appeal to the experience I get when I touch the apple: that's what we're trying to explain. Unsupported phenomenalism simply gives no explanation for the action-experience connections. On this view, the regularities are just brute facts. The truth of the principle of informative experience, on this interpretation, seems to be just an accident.

---

18. Andrew Baxter, *Nature of the Human Soul*, 2:284.

Something like unsupported phenomenalism was to be defended a century later by John Stuart Mill. It is not a tenable interpretation of Berkeley.

3.4 Theistic Phenomenalism

We distinguished above between two roles that Berkeley attributes to God: that of perceiving things when no one else is around to do the job and that of determining which action-experience connections prevail.

With the move from ordinary things to sensible qualities, the first role has become unnecessary. An example will make this point: Suppose I am standing in front of a brick wall. If I run forward, I will break my nose. A benevolent God will want to make it clear to me that this action-experience connection prevails. To do this, all he has to do is to cause me to have an idea of a brick wall. It really does not matter whether or not he also has this idea as long as he always produces this idea in me whenever this action-experience connection prevails. In other words, God's intentions and actions matter to us, while his experiences are of no more interest or relevance to an account of perceptual knowledge than the undetectable properties of the New Philosophers' material substance.

Berkeley was aware that it is God's intentions that matter for our lives, and not any ideas he may or may not have. In the passage quoted in the section on continuous realism, he acknowledges that it is not enough for God to know or comprehend the order of nature. God must also *cause* us to have the appropriate ideas at the appropriate times. In the *Third Dialogue*, Hylas is puzzled about how Philonous can account for the creation on his principles. Philonous responds to his question by explaining,

> Things, with regard to us, may properly be said to begin their existence, or be created, when God decreed they should become perceptible to intelligent creatures, in that order and manner which he then established, and we now call the laws of Nature.[19]

Thus it is God's decision to cause ideas in us according to a uniform pattern that accounts for the existence of things.

---

19. *Third Dialogue*, p. 84.

Theistic phenomenalism, unlike unsupported phenomenalism, allows Berkeley to give an explanation of the action-experience connections. These connections are established by God. They are an expression of his benevolence for they allow our experience to provide a guide for our action. So, the principle of informative experience is ultimately explained by God's role in the production of our ideas and his benevolence. A benevolent God would not produce ideas in us in a chaotic manner.

This conception gives Berkeley an account of empirical knowledge that does not rely on the material objects of the New Philosophy and which is therefore immune to the skeptical problems that the New Philosophers faced. It also provides the basis for an immaterialist reply to worries about the uniformity of nature. We can trust that, if we discover regularities that are the reflection of divine intentions, they will continue to prevail in the future. God's stable intentions underwrite the principle of informative experience, and they allow us to make use of past and present experience in anticipating the future. Thus God is moved to the center of Berkeley's philosophical system.

For many, this lessens the system's philosophical appeal. But it enhances its plausibility as an interpretation of Berkeley — for he clearly conceived of God as playing a central role in his metaphysics.

3.5 Interpreting Berkeley

Which of these interpretations is the correct interpretation of Berkeley's philosophy? This is a complicated question, and the reader should consult some of the articles in the bibliography to get a rounded view of the controversies. It is safe to say that any interpretation of Berkeley's philosophy that does not provide a large role for God does not adequately represent his intentions. This principle eliminates both discontinuous realism and unsupported phenomenalism. Although both these views have been attributed to Berkeley and although Berkeley's writings have played a role in leading some philosophers to hold these views themselves, they are not adequate as accounts of Berkeley's own thinking.

We are left with the two theistic views, continuous realism and theistic phenomenalism. If we were forced to choose one of these as the best interpretation of Berkeley, we would choose the latter. But this choice is partly based on Berkeley's writings other than the *Three Dialogues* and by the fact that we find theistic phenomenalism the more attractive of the two theories. In the *Three Dialogues*, elements of both views are to be found.

We think that in the *Three Dialogues* Berkeley's basic view is theistic phenomenalism. On this view, we immediately perceive only sensible qualities and combinations of sensible qualities, not ordinary things. We have inferential knowledge of patterns in our perceptions of sensible qualities and of action-experience connections. God's role is to have stable intentions about patterns of connection between action and experience and to carry these intentions out. For sensible qualities, to be is to be perceived. There is no possibility of mistake in a perception of a sensible quality. We can, however, be mistaken in our inferential knowledge of the patterns that connect different sensible qualities.

In spite of his basic commitment to theistic phenomenalism, Berkeley tried to make his view as compatible with common sense and ordinary speech as possible. This is especially true in the *Dialogues*. Theistic phenomenalism does not, on the face of it, have any place for ordinary things as enduring wholes. In an attempt to solve this difficulty, Berkeley tended to identify ordinary objects with combinations of sensible qualities. This identification attempts to preserve our ordinary talk of trees and tables without admitting that there is any more to such things than the sensible ideas to which theistic phenomenalism is committed. This identification also serves a useful role in the argument of the *Dialogues*, since it allows him at points to shift from talk about sensible things in the sense of trees and such to talk about sensible things in the sense of sensible qualities. This shift allows him to use the arguments of the New Philosophers to show that sensible ideas exist only in the mind and also that, for ordinary things, to be is to be perceived. This shift in the use of "sensible qualities" confuses many readers, and it may have confused Berkeley himself.

But even if Berkeley thought about ordinary things in this way some of the time, the view that ordinary things are combinations of ideas won't work, as long as sensible ideas meet the "to be is to be perceived" criterion. Part of what is involved in the idea of an ordinary thing is that it is possible for it to be perceived by different people and to be observed at different times and in different ways. You and I can both see the same tree; I can look at the same tree on different occasions; and we can touch and smell the tree as well as see it. So, if the tree is to be a combination of sensible ideas, the combination will have to include ideas from different observers and different sensory modalities. But such a combination would include incompatible ideas of the tree — say, the idea of a particular small size obtained from a distant view and the idea of a much larger size obtained from a closer look. But trees and other ordinary things can only have one size and, for all Berkeley's rhetoric, he cannot reconcile theistic phenomenalism with ordinary talk of ordinary things.

Theistic phenomenalism can provide an analysis of our belief that things continue to exist when unperceived. What continues to exist is God's intention to cause certain experiences given certain actions. It would even be consistent with theistic phenomenalism to go further and to suppose that God continues to have ideas of sensible qualities in addition to these continued intentions. Berkeley may well have supposed this, although doing so would raise a number of problems. All of this does not add up to the continued existence of ordinary things, however. Ideas are not ordinary things because ordinary things can be perceived by different people at different times and places, and people can make mistakes about them. In common sense, ordinary objects serve to explain action-experience connections. A certain movement will lead to a certain taste in my mouth because there is an apple appropriately located. In theistic phenomenalism, the only explanation of the link is God.

Theistic phenomenalism is an interesting, original, and influential view that gives Berkeley most of what he wants. But it cannot fulfill Berkeley's dream of providing a new foundation for common sense.

4. Berkeley's Life and Works

George Berkeley was born on March 12, 1685 in Kilkenny, Ireland.[20] His family was of English origin and appears to have come to Ireland following the Restoration. Little is known of his early life except that his family was moderately prosperous and were Protestant, as were most Irish of English descent.

---

[20] The best and only modern biography of Berkeley is *The Life of George Berkeley, Bishop of Cloyne,* by A. A. Luce. A more detailed account of Berkeley's American connections can be found in *George Berkeley in America,* by Edmond Gaustad. The facts in our brief sketch of Berkeley's life are largely drawn from these two books.

Berkeley entered Trinity College, Dublin in 1700 at the age of 15. The education he received there was progressive in several respects and included a selection of modern philosophers. Especially important for the future philosopher was Locke's *Essay* and works of other New Philosophers including Descartes and Malebranche. Berkeley received his B.A. in 1704 and was elected to a Junior Fellowship in 1707. As his fellowship required, he was ordained as an Anglican minister in 1710. His official connection with the college continued until he was appointed Dean of Derry in 1724.

The central ideas of his immaterialist philosophy are clearly stated in notebooks that he kept in the years immediately following his election as fellow; the most important of Berkeley's philosophical works were published while he was in still in his twenties. The first of Berkeley's philosophically significant publications was *An essay towards a new theory of vision* which was published in 1709. This was followed in 1710 by *A treatise concerning the principle of human knowledge*, Part I.[21] The *Three Dialogues between Hylas and Philonous* which covers much of the same material as *The Principles* was published in 1713. These three books contain the essential elements of Berkeley's immaterialism, a view which he was to hold without major modification till the end of his life.

The first of these works, the *New Theory of Vision*, contains Berkeley's attempt to provide a theory of the visual perception of depth. Berkeley argues that distance is not immediately perceived via sight, although it is immediately perceived using touch. All we can immediately perceive visually is the two-dimensional arrangement of objects, not their distance from us. This far, Berkeley agreed with many of his contemporaries. But Berkeley goes further, arguing that the spatial properties perceived by sight are not even the same properties as those gained from touch. In an important metaphor, Berkeley compares visual ideas to a language; they serve as the *signs* of the spatial ideas correlated with them. It is the regular connection between the two kinds of ideas that allows vision to provide us information about the distance of the objects we perceive, not any similarity between the ideas of vision and touch. Berkeley's theory of

---

21. Berkeley completed a draft of Part II but lost the manuscript while travelling in Italy and never attempted to recreate it.

vision is, in several important respects, a special case of his general phenomenalism restricted to the analysis of visual perception of space.

The *New Theory of Vision* was the most successful of Berkeley's early works, going through two editions in its first year. It gained a reputation for Berkeley both in England and in the rest of Europe and was regarded as an important contribution to the study of vision. Berkeley's other early works were less favorably treated by the reading public. *The principles of human knowledge* is Berkeley's most complete and detailed statement of immaterialism. To say that it was unfavorably received would be to understate its complete failure. It seems to have been widely known but little read and was chiefly the object of ridicule. One of Berkeley's friends, in describing the reaction to it in London, reports that, "A physician of my acquaintance. . . argued you must needs be mad, and that you ought to take remedies."[22]

Berkeley did not give up on gaining an audience for his immaterialism. *The Three Dialogues* is Berkeley's attempt to express the fundamental ideas of immaterialism in a style more accessible to the general public. He also attempted to make clear in this work his complete opposition to the skepticism which was attributed to him on the basis of *The principles*. Although his second attempt at expressing his great philosophical insight was better received than the first, it still failed to generate any serious discussion. Not until well after his death was Berkeley's philosophy to receive any serious philosophical attention.

Berkeley himself, when he came to London to see *The Dialogues* through the press, received a much better reception than had his books. His friends and acquaintances included such leading literary figures of the time as Swift, Pope, Addison, and Steele. From 1713 till 1721, Berkeley spent his time either in London, where he was engaged in various literary enterprises, or in several tours of continental Europe. He was promoted to Senior Fellow at Trinity College in his absence. He published *De Motu*, an application of his immaterialist principles to problems of motion, in 1721. Berkeley also published *An Essay towards preventing the ruine of Great Britain* (1721) in which he expressed his disgust with the current state of culture and morality in England, an evaluation which was shortly to have

---

22. Letter from Percival, quoted in Luce, p. 50.

important consequences. Late in 1721 Berkeley returned to Ireland with the hope of obtaining a position within the Irish Anglican church.

On his return to Ireland, Berkeley resumed his active association with Trinity College and started the complicated political process of obtaining a preferment within the Irish church. After some false hopes and complicated negotiations, he was appointed Dean of Derry in 1724. His deanship carried no responsibilities and provided him with a large income. Both of these attributes were important, since they together allowed him to embark seriously on a major project that he had been contemplating for several years — the founding of a college in America.

Sometime soon after writing his essay on the deplorable state of British civilization, Berkeley formed the plan of founding a college in Bermuda. With the decline of Europe, the only hope for the future of civilization lay in the British colonies in America. Berkeley proposed to do his part by moving to Bermuda and organizing a college for the education of both British colonists and Native Americans from the mainland. The spirit of the Bermuda project is nicely expressed in a poem Berkeley wrote at this time:

America or The Muse's Refuge
A Prophecy

The Muse, disgusted at an Age and Clime,
Barren of every glorious Theme,
In distant Lands now waits a better Time,
Producing subjects worthy Fame:

In happy Climes, where from the genial Sun
And virgin Earth such Scenes ensue,
The Force of Art by Nature seems outdone,
And fancied Beauties by the true:

There shall be sung another golden Age,
The rise of Empire and of Arts,
The Good and Great inspiring epic Rage,
The wisest Heads and noblest Hearts.

Not such as *Europe* breeds in her decay;
    Such as she bred when fresh and young,
When heav'nly Flame did animate her Clay,
    By future Poets shall be sung.

Westward the Course of Empire takes its Way;
    The four first Acts already past,
A fifth shall close the Drama with the Day;
    Time's noblest Offspring is the last.

In 1724 Berkeley published *A Proposal For the better Supplying of Churches in our Foreign Plantations, and for Converting the Savage American to Christianity.* In this tract, he laid out in considerable detail the plans for St. Paul's College in Bermuda. He spent the next few years raising money and political support for his project. By 1726, he had succeeded in raising a substantial sum privately, the vote of parliament for a much larger amount, and a royal charter for his new college. He had also managed to secure the agreement in principle of a number of scholars, drawn disproportionately from his Trinity College colleagues, to form the nucleus of the faculty of the Bermuda college. By 1728, however, the Bermuda project had aroused considerable opposition and there were serious doubts about his ever obtaining the funds from the parliamentary grant. Berkeley had also come to realize that Bermuda, located 600 miles from the mainland and lacking adequate supplies of food and water, was not an ideal location for an institution of higher learning. In hope of forcing parliament's hand and also of finding a better location for the college, he set sail for Newport, Rhode Island, in the fall of 1728. Shortly before leaving, Berkeley married Anne Forster of Dublin who accompanied him to Newport.

Berkeley spent three years in Newport and, although he never succeeded in founding his college, the venture was not a total loss. At the time of Berkeley's visit, there was no Anglican bishop in the colonies, the Bishop of London had jurisdiction, and Berkeley was the highest ranking ecclesiastic to venture to the British colonies. Berkeley was also the first philosopher and literary figure of any note to visit America. As such, he had a substantial impact on the philosophical life of the colonies. The first sustained and serious criticism of immaterialism was provided by a Connecticut clergyman and philosopher, Samuel Johnson, who met

Berkeley in Newport and continued to correspond with him till his death. Johnson, who was one of the very few converts to immaterialism in Berkeley's lifetime, went on to become the first president of Columbia University in New York. Johnson also wrote the first American philosophy textbook, *Elementa Philosophica*, which was published by Benjamin Franklin in 1752 and was dedicated to Berkeley.

While in Newport, Berkeley wrote his first major philosophical work after the *Three Dialogues*, another set of dialogues titled *Alciphron*. In it, he attempted to refute what he saw as the irreligious views popular among literary figures of his time. *Alciphron*, published in 1732, touched on some of the same issues as Berkeley's earlier metaphysical books, but was primarily concerned with defending Christian doctrine. The setting for *Alciphron* is recognizably Newport, and the book's impact was greater in the New World than in the Old. Jonathan Edwards read *Alciphron* within a year of its publication, and the influence of immaterialism can be detected in many of his writings.

In spite of Berkeley's intellectual successes in America, the project of founding a college was dying. In 1731, he had the Bishop of London press the Prime Minister, Robert Walpole, on whether the parliamentary grant would be paid. Walpole replied,

> If you put the question to me as a Minister, I must and I can assure you that the money shall most undoubtedly be paid as soon as suits with public convenience; but if you ask me as a friend whether Dean Berkeley should continue in America, expecting the payment of £20,000, I advise him by all means to return home to Europe. [23]

Later in 1731, Berkeley returned to England by way of Boston, his grand dream a failure.

Berkeley's connection with the American colonies did not end with his return to Europe. Before leaving, he donated the house and farm he had purchased in Newport to Yale University.[24] On his return, he used the funds he had raised privately for the Bermuda project to purchase books

---

23. Luce, p. 142.
24. Berkeley's house, Whitehall, is still standing and can be visited during the summer.

for the Yale and Harvard libraries. The donation of books to Yale was particularly large, approximately 1000 volumes, and at the time represented a 50% increase in the library's holdings. He also arranged for an organ to be purchased for Trinity Church, Newport. Berkeley, California, the home of the University of California, was named after Berkeley, although not primarily because of his philosophical accomplishments. Berkeley's views on the westward flow of civilization were known to the developers of America's western frontier, and it was a railroad magnate, Frederick Billings, who received the inspiration to name the new university town after Berkeley.

On his return to England Berkeley busied himself with seeing *Alciphron* through publication and with the composition of a short tract defending his theory of vision, *The Theory of Vision. . . Vindicated and Explained* (1733). He also published an attack on the coherence of Newton's version of the calculus, *The Analyst or a discourse addressed to an infidel mathematician* (1734). This tract aroused a great deal of discussion and was the occasion of several polemics on both sides. In addition to his literary endeavors, he was engaged in attempting to secure a promotion within the church hierarchy. In 1734, Berkeley was appointed Bishop of Cloyne, a somewhat obscure bishopric in the south of Ireland near Cork. Berkeley was to spend the rest of his life in Cloyne, except for a few months shortly before his death.

With his arrival in Cloyne, the great events of Berkeley's life were over. Although he continued to maintain an active correspondence, with two notable exceptions, his career as a public figure was finished. Most of his time he devoted to his pastoral duties and to his family life. His writings of this period are primarily addressed more to practical issues than to metaphysical ones.

Berkeley's circle of friends included a group who promoted a form of moderate Irish nationalism and he was sympathetic to their cause. Berkeley published *The Querist* (1735-37) as his contribution to the attempt to persuade the English to change their policy towards Ireland. *The Querist* is rather peculiar in form, consisting entirely of questions. In spite of the work's interrogative nature, Berkeley's diagnosis of the causes of Irish poverty comes through clearly: an unhealthy combination of English greed and Irish sloth.

Berkeley's last significant appearance on the public scene involved both his concern with practical affairs and his bent for philosophical speculation. In 1744 he published *Siris, Philosophical Reflexions and inquiries concerning the virtues of tar-water, and divers other subjects connected together and arising from one another*. The early 1740's were a period of famine and epidemic in Ireland, and there were no physicians in Berkeley's diocese. Berkeley took it upon himself to do what he could for the sick and settled upon tar-water as the best malady for the various ailments that he treated. He prepared tar-water by mixing pine tar with water, allowing it to settle, and then draining off the clear fluid for medicinal use. *Siris*, which starts with a discussion of the virtues of tar-water for curing most diseases, was the most popular of his books during his lifetime. It was widely read on the continent and in America and quickly went through several editions. Most of its readers, however, read it for its medical discussions and ignored its main subject, a chain of philosophical reflections that start with tar and end with the Trinity. In *Siris*, Berkeley restated many of the tenets of the immaterialism of his youth but mixed them with even more speculative ideas, drawing heavily on classical works. The end result is the most difficult of Berkeley's works to read, although one with significant philosophical content. This poem captures the spirit of the work as a whole:

On tar

Hail vulgar juice of never-fading pine!
Cheap as thou art, thy virtues are divine.
To shew them and explain (such is thy store)
There needs much modern and much ancient lore.
While with slow pains we search the healing spell,
Those sparks of life, that in thy balsam dwell,
From lowest earth by gentle steps we rise
Through air, fire, æther to the highest skies.
Things gross and low present truth's sacred clue.
Sense, fancy reason, intellect pursue
Her winding mazes, and by Nature's laws
From plain effects trace out the mystic cause,
And principles explore, though wrapt in shades,
That spring of life which the great world pervades,
The spirit that moves, the Intellect that guides,
Th' eternal One that o'er the Whole presides.
Go learn'd mechanic, stare with stupid eyes,

Attribute to all figure, weight and size;
Nor look behind the moving scene to see
What gives each wondrous form its energy.
Vain images possess the sensual mind,
To real agents and true causes blind.
But soon as intellect's bright sun displays
O'er the benighted orb his fulgent rays,
Delusive phantoms fly before the light,
Nature and truth lie open at the sight:
Causes connect with effects supply
A golden chain, whose radiant links on high
Fix'd to the sovereign throne from thence depend
And reach e'en down to tar the nether end.

The rest of Berkeley's life was uneventful. There was talk from time to time of promoting Berkeley to a better diocese, but he never pursued these opportunities. In 1752, he traveled to Oxford to oversee the education of his son George. He was in poor health when he left Ireland, and after five months in Oxford he died, apparently of a stroke. His will specified that he be buried in the churchyard of the parish in which he died; he was buried in Christ Church, Oxford on January 20, 1753.

5. A Note on the Text

The text of the dialogues is based on the edition of 1734. This edition was the last revised by Berkeley and contained significant changes from the first edition of 1713. The more important of the differences between the two editions are indicated by the use of square brackets. The spelling has been modernized and changed to conform to American standards. A few changes in Berkeley's punctuation and the correction of a very few obvious misprints have been made in the interests of clarity. With these exceptions the language in this edition is Berkeley's own.

Selected Bibliography

Works by Berkeley

Luce, A. A., and Jessop, T. E. (eds.), *The Works of George Berkeley, Bishop of Cloyne*, 9 volumes. London: Nelson, 1948-57.
Winkler, Kenneth, *A Treatise Concerning the Principles of Human Knowledge*. Indianapolis: Hackett Publishing Company, 1982.

Anthologies on Berkeley

Martin, C. B., and Armstrong, David (eds.), *Locke and Berkeley*. Garden City, New York: Doubleday, 1968; Notre Dame: University of Notre Dame Press.
Turbayne, Colin Murray (ed.), *A Treatise Concerning the Principles of Human Knowledge / George Berkeley, with Critical Essays*. Indianapolis: Bobbs-Merrill, 1970.
Turbayne, Colin Murray (ed.), *Berkeley; Critical and Interpretive Essays*. Minneapolis: University of Minnesota Press, 1982.

Books and Articles on Berkeley

Adams, Robert M., "Berkeley's 'Notion' of Spiritual Substance," *Archiv für Geschicte der Philosophie* 55 (1973), pp. 47-69.
Gaustad, Edwin S., *George Berkeley in America*. New Haven: Yale University Press, 1979.
Grayling, A. C., *Berkeley: The Central Arguments*. La Salle, Illinois: Open Court, 1986.
Luce, A. A., *Berkeley and Malebranche*. Oxford: Oxford University Press, 1934.
Luce, A. A., *Berkeley's Immaterialism*. London: Nelson, 1945.
Luce, A. A., *The Dialectic of Immaterialism*. London: Hodder and Stoughton, 1963.
Luce, A. A., *The Life of George Berkeley, Bishop of Cloyne*. London: Nelson, 1949.
Pitcher, George, *Berkeley*. London: Routledge & Kegan Paul, 1977.
Popkin, Richard H., "Berkeley and Pyrrhonism," *Review of Metaphysics*

5(1951), pp. 223-46. Reprinted in Popkin, *The High Road to Pyrrhonism*, pp. 297-318.

Popkin, Richard H., "Berkeley's Influence on American Philosophy," *Hermathena* 82 (1953), pp. 128-146. Reprinted in Popkin, *The High Road to Pyrrhonism*, pp. 339-353.

Popkin, Richard H., "The New Realism of Bishop Berkeley," in Popkin, *The High Road to Pyrrhonism*, pp. 319-338.

Tipton, Ian C., *Berkeley: The Philosophy of Immaterialism*. London: Methuen, 1974.

Winkler, Kenneth P., *Berkeley: An Interpretation*. Oxford: Oxford University Press, 1989.

Other Works of Interest

Bayle, Pierre, *Historical and Critical Dictionary: Selections*, translated with an introduction and notes by Richard Popkin. Indianapolis: Bobbs-Merrill, 1965.

Descartes, Rene, *Discourse on Method* and *Meditations on First Philosophy*, translated by Donald A. Cress. Indianapolis: Hackett Publishing Company, 1980.

Locke, John, *An Essay concerning Human Understanding*, edited with an introduction by Peter H. Nidditch. Oxford: Oxford University Press, 1975

Popkin, Richard H., *The High Road to Pyrrhonism*. San Diego: Austin Hill Press, 1980.

Three Dialogues *between* *Hylas and Philonous*

The design of which is plainly to demonstrate the reality and perfection of human knowledge, the incorporeal nature of the soul, and the immediate providence of a Deity: in opposition to Sceptics and Atheists. Also to open a method for rendering the Sciences more easy, useful, and compendious.

DEDICATION
TO THE RIGHT HONOURABLE

THE LORD BERKELEY OF STRATTON

MASTER OF THE ROLLS IN THE KINDOM OF IRELAND,
CHANCELLOR OF THE DUCHY OF LANCASTER, AND ONE
OF THE LORDS OF HER MAJESTY'S MOST HONOURABLE
PRIVY-COUNCIL

My Lord,

The virtue, learning, and good sense, which are acknowledged to distinguish your character, would tempt me to indulge myself the pleasure men naturally take, in giving applause to those, whom they esteem and honour: and it should seem of importance to the subjects of Great Britain, that they knew, the eminent share you enjoy in the favour of your Sovereign, and the honours she has conferred upon you, have not been owing to any application from Your Lordship, but entirely to Her Majesty's own thought, arising from a sense of your personal merit, and an inclination to reward it. But as your name is prefixed to this treatise, with an intention to do honour to myself alone, I shall only say, that I am encouraged, by the favour you have treated me with, to address these papers to Your Lordship. And I was the more ambitious of doing this, because a philosophical treatise could not so properly be addressed to any one, as to a person of Your Lordship's character, who, to your other valuable distinctions, have added the knowledge and relish of philosophy. I am, with the greatest respect,

My Lord,
Your Lordship's most obedient, and
most humble servant,
George Berkeley

THE PREFACE

Though it seems the general opinion of the world, no less than the design of Nature and Providence, that the end of speculation be practice, or the improvement and regulation of our lives and actions; yet those, who are most addicted to speculative studies, seem as generally of another mind. And, indeed, if we consider the pains that have been taken, to perplex the plainest things, that distrust of the senses, those doubts and scruples, those abstractions and refinements that occur in the very entrance of the sciences; it will not seem strange, that men of leisure and curiosity should lay themselves out in fruitless disquisitions, without descending to the practical parts of life, or informing themselves in the more necessary and important parts of knowledge.

Upon the common principles of philosophers, we are not assured of the existence of things from their being perceived. And we are taught to distinguish their real nature from that which falls under our senses. Hence arise *skepticism* and *paradoxes*. It is not enough, that we see and feel, that we taste and smell a thing. Its true nature, its absolute external entity, is still concealed. For, though it be the fiction of our own brain, we have made it inaccessible to all our faculties. Sense is fallacious, reason defective. We spend our lives in doubting of those things which other men evidently know, and believing those things which they laugh at, and despise.

In order, therefore, to divert the busy mind of man from vain researches, it seemed necessary to inquire into the source of its perplexities; and, if possible, to lay down such principles, as, by an easy solution of them, together with their own native evidence, may, at once, recommend themselves for genuine to the mind, and rescue it from those endless pursuits it is engaged in. Which, with a plain demonstration of the immediate Providence of an all-seeing God, and the natural immortality of the soul, should seem the readiest preparation, as well as the strongest motive, to the study and practice of virtue.

This design I proposed, in the First Part of a Treatise concerning the *Principles of Human Knowledge*, published in the year 1710. But, before I proceed to publish the Second Part, I thought it requisite to treat more clearly and fully of certain principles laid down in the First, and to place them in a new light. Which is the business of the following *Dialogues*.

In this treatise, which does not presuppose in the reader, any knowledge of what was contained in the former, it has been my aim to introduce the notions I advance, into the mind, in the most easy and familiar manner; especially, because they carry with them a great opposition to the prejudices of philosophers, which have so far prevailed against the common sense and natural notions of mankind.

If the principles, which I here endeavor to propagate, are admitted for true; the consequences which, I think, evidently flow from thence, are, that *atheism* and *skepticism* will be utterly destroyed, many intricate points made plain, great difficulties solved, several useless parts of science retrenched, speculation referred to practice, and men reduced from paradoxes to common sense.

And although it may, perhaps, seem an uneasy reflection to some, that when they have taken a circuit through so many refined and unvulgar notions, they should at last come to think like other men: yet, methinks, this return to the simple dictates of Nature, after having wandered through the wild mazes of philosophy, is not unpleasant. It is like coming home from a long voyage: a man reflects with pleasure on the many difficulties and perplexities he has passed through, sets his heart at ease, and enjoys himself with more satisfaction for the future.

As it was my intention to convince *skeptics* and *infidels* by reason, so it has been my endeavor strictly to observe the most rigid laws of reasoning. And, to an impartial reader, I hope, it will be manifest, that the sublime notion of a God, and the comfortable expectation of immortality, do naturally arise from a close and methodical application of thought: whatever may be the result of that loose, rambling way, not altogether improperly termed *free-thinking*, by certain libertines in thought, who can no more endure the restraints of *logic*, than those of *religion*, or *government*.

It will, perhaps, be objected to my design, that so far as it tends to ease the mind of difficult and useless inquiries, it can affect only a few speculative persons; but, if by their speculations rightly placed, the study of morality and the Law of Nature were brought more into fashion among men of parts and genius, the discouragements that draw to *skepticism* removed, the measures of right and wrong accurately defined, and the principles of natural religion reduced into regular systems, as artfully disposed and clearly connected as those of some other sciences: there are grounds to think, these effects would not only have a gradual influence in repairing the too much defaced sense of virtue in the world; but also, by showing, that such parts of revelation, as lie within the reach of human inquiry, are most agreeable to right reason, would dispose all prudent unprejudiced persons, to a modest and wary treatment of those sacred mysteries, which are above the comprehension of our faculties.

It remains, that I desire the reader to withhold his censure of these *Dialogues*, till he has read them through. Otherwise, he may lay them aside in a mistake of their design, or on account of difficulties or objections which he would find answered in the sequel. A treatise of this nature would require to be once read over coherently, in order to comprehend its design, the proofs, solution of difficulties, and the connection and disposition of its parts. If it be thought to deserve a second reading; this, I imagine, will make the entire scheme very plain: especially, if recourse be had to an Essay I wrote, some years since, upon *Vision*, and the Treatise concerning the *Principles of Human Knowledge*. Wherein divers notions advanced in these *Dialogues*, are farther pursued, or placed in different lights, and other points handled, which naturally tend to confirm and illustrate them.

THE FIRST DIALOGUE

Philonous. Good morrow, Hylas: I did not expect to find you abroad so early.

Hylas. It is indeed something unusual; but my thoughts were so taken up with a subject I was discoursing of last night, that finding I could not sleep, I resolved to rise and take a turn in the garden.

Phil. It happened well, to let you see what innocent and agreeable pleasures you lose every morning. Can there be a pleasanter time of the day, or a more delightful season of the year? That purple sky, those wild but sweet notes of birds, the fragrant bloom upon the trees and flowers, the gentle influence of the rising sun, these and a thousand nameless beauties of nature inspire the soul with secret transports; its faculties too being at this time fresh and lively, are fit for those meditations, which the solitude of a garden and tranquility of the morning naturally dispose us to. But I am afraid I interrupt your thoughts: for you seemed very intent on something.

Hyl. It is true, I was, and shall be obliged to you if you will permit me to go on in the same vein; not that I would by any means deprive myself of your company, for my thoughts always flow more easily in conversation with a friend, than when I am alone: but my request is, that you would suffer me to impart my reflections to you.

Phil. With all my heart, it is what I should have requested myself if you had not prevented me.

Hyl. I was considering the odd fate of those men who have in all ages, through an affectation of being distinguished from the vulgar, or some unaccountable turn of thought, pretended either to believe nothing at all, or to believe the most extravagant things in the world. This however might be borne, if their paradoxes and skepticism did not draw after them some consequences of general disadvantage to mankind. But the mischief lies here; that when men of less leisure see them who are supposed to have spent their whole time in the pursuits of knowledge professing an entire ignorance of all things, or advancing such notions as are repugnant to plain and commonly received principles, they will be tempted to entertain suspicions concerning the most important truths, which they had hitherto held sacred and unquestionable.

Phil. I entirely agree with you, as to the ill tendency of the affected doubts of some philosophers, and fantastical conceits of others.

I am even so far gone of late in this way of thinking, that I have quitted several of the sublime notions I had got in their schools for vulgar opinions. And I give it you on my word; since this revolt from metaphysical notions to the plain dictates of nature and common sense, I find my understanding strangely enlightened, so that I can now easily comprehend a great many things which before were all mystery and riddle.

Hyl.   I am glad to find there was nothing in the accounts I heard of you.

Phil.   Pray, what were those?

Hyl.   You were represented, in last night's conversation, as one who maintained the most extravagant opinion that ever entered into the mind of man, to wit, that there is no such thing as *material substance* in the world.

Phil.   That there is no such thing as what philosophers call *material substance*, I am seriously persuaded: but, if I were made to see anything absurd or skeptical in this, I should then have the same reason to renounce this, that I imagine I have now to reject the contrary opinion.

Hyl.   What! Can anything be more fantastical, more repugnant to common sense, or a more manifest piece of skepticism, than to believe there is no such thing as *matter*?

Phil.   Softly, good Hylas. What if it should prove that you, who hold there is, are, by virtue of that opinion, a greater *skeptic*, and maintain more paradoxes and repugnances to common sense, than I who believe no such thing?

Hyl.   You may as soon persuade me, the part is greater than the whole, as that, in order to avoid absurdity and skepticism, I should ever be obliged to give up my opinion in this point.

Phil.   Well then, are you content to admit that opinion for true, which upon examination shall appear most agreeable to common sense, and remote from skepticism?

Hyl.   With all my heart. Since you are for raising disputes about the plainest things in nature, I am content for once to hear what you have to say.

Phil.   Pray, Hylas, what do you mean by a *skeptic*?

Hyl.   I mean what all men mean, one that doubts of everything.

Phil.   He then who entertains no doubt concerning some particular point, with regard to that point cannot be thought a *skeptic*.

Hyl.   I agree with you.

Phil. Whether does doubting consist, in embracing the affirmative or negative side of a question?

Hyl. In neither; for whoever understands English cannot but know that *doubting* signifies a suspense between both.

Phil. He then that denies any point, can no more be said to doubt of it, than he who affirms it with the same degree of assurance.

Hyl. True.

Phil. And, consequently, for such his denial is no more to be esteemed a *skeptic* than the other.

Hyl. I acknowledge it.

Phil. How comes it then, Hylas, that you pronounce me a *skeptic*, because I deny what you affirm, to wit, the existence of Matter? Since, for aught you can tell, I am as peremptory in my denial, as you in your affirmation.

Hyl. Hold, Philonous, I have been a little out in my definition; but every false step a man makes in discourse is not to be insisted on. I said indeed that a *skeptic* was one who doubted of everything; but I should have added, or who denies the reality and truth of things.

Phil. What things? Do you mean the principles and theorems of sciences? But these you know are universal intellectual notions, and consequently independent of matter. The denial therefore of this does not imply the denying them.

Hyl. I grant it. But are there no other things? What think you of distrusting the senses, of denying the real existence of sensible things, or pretending to know nothing of them. Is not this sufficient to denominate a man a *skeptic*?

Phil. Shall we therefore examine which of us it is that denies the reality of sensible things, or professes the greatest ignorance of them; since, if I take you rightly, he is to be esteemed the greatest *skeptic*?

Hyl. That is what I desire.

Phil. What mean you by sensible things?

Hyl. Those things which are perceived by the senses. Can you imagine that I mean anything else?

Phil. Pardon me, Hylas, if I am desirous clearly to apprehend your notions, since this may much shorten our inquiry. Suffer me then to ask you this farther question. Are those things only perceived by the senses which are perceived immediately? Or, may those things properly be said to be sensible which are perceived mediately or not without the intervention of others?

Hyl. I do not sufficiently understand you.

Phil. In reading a book, what I immediately perceive are the letters; but mediately, or by means of these, are suggested to my mind the notions of God, virtue, truth, &c. Now, that the letters are truly sensible things, or perceived by sense, there is no doubt: but I would know whether you take the things suggested by them to be so too.

Hyl. No, certainly: it were absurd to think *God* or *virtue* sensible things; though they may be signified and suggested to the mind by sensible marks, with which they have an arbitrary connection.

Phil. It seems then, that by *sensible things* you mean those only which can be perceived immediately by sense?

Hyl. Right.

Phil. Does it not follow from this, that though I see one part of the sky red, and another blue, and that my reason does thence evidently conclude there must be some cause of that diversity of colors, yet that cause cannot be said to be a sensible thing, or perceived by the sense of seeing?

Hyl. It does.

Phil. In like manner, though I hear variety of sounds, yet I cannot be said to hear the causes of those sounds?

Hyl. You cannot.

Phil. And when by my touch I perceive a thing to be hot and heavy, I cannot say, with any truth or propriety, that I feel the cause of its heat or weight?

Hyl. To prevent any more questions of this kind, I tell you once for all, that by *sensible things* I mean those only which are perceived by sense, and that in truth the senses perceive nothing which they do not perceive immediately: for they make no inferences. The deducing therefore of causes or occasions from effects and appearances, which alone are perceived by sense, entirely relates to reason.

Phil. This point then is agreed between us, that *sensible things are those only which are immediately perceived by sense.* You will farther inform me, whether we immediately perceive by sight anything beside light, and colors, and figures: or by hearing, anything but sounds: by the palate, anything beside tastes: by the smell, beside odors: or by the touch, more than tangible qualities.

Hyl.   We do not.

Phil.   It seems, therefore, that if you take away all sensible qualities, there remains nothing sensible?

Hyl.   I grant it.

Phil.   Sensible things therefore are nothing else but so many sensible qualities, or combinations of sensible qualities?

Hyl.   Nothing else.

Phil.   Heat then is a sensible thing?

Hyl.   Certainly.

Phil.   Does the reality of sensible things consist in being perceived? Or, is it something distinct from their being perceived, and that bears no relation to the mind?

Hyl.   To *exist* is one thing, and to be *perceived* is another.

Phil.   I speak with regard to sensible things only: and of these I ask, whether by their real existence you mean a subsistence exterior to the mind, and distinct from their being perceived?

Hyl.   I mean a real absolute being, distinct from, and without any relation to, their being perceived.

Phil.   Heat therefore, if it be allowed a real being, must exist without the mind?

Hyl.   It must.

Phil.   Tell me, Hylas, is this real existence equally compatible to all degrees of heat, which we perceive: or is there any reason why we should attribute it to some, and deny it to others? And if there be, pray let me know that reason.

Hyl.   Whatever degree of heat we perceive by sense, we may be sure the same exists in the object that occasions it.

Phil.   What, the greatest as well as the least?

Hyl.   I tell you, the reason is plainly the same in respect of both: they are both perceived by sense; nay, the greater degree of heat is more sensibly perceived; and consequently, if there is any difference, we are more certain of its real existence than we can be of the reality of a lesser degree.

Phil.   But is not the most vehement and intense degree of heat a very great pain?

Hyl.   No one can deny it.

Phil.   And is any unperceiving thing capable of pain or pleasure?

Hyl.   No certainly.

Phil.   Is your material substance a senseless being, or a being endowed with sense and perception?

Hyl.   It is senseless, without doubt.

Phil.   It cannot therefore be the subject of pain?

Hyl.   By no means.

Phil.   Nor consequently of the greatest heat perceived by sense, since you acknowledge this to be no small pain?

Hyl.   I grant it.

Phil.   What shall we say then of your external object; is it a material substance, or no?

Hyl.   It is a material substance with the sensible qualities inhering in it.

Phil.   How then can a great heat exist in it, since you own it cannot in a material substance? I desire you would clear this point.

Hyl.   Hold, Philonous, I fear I was out in yielding intense heat to be a pain. It should seem rather, that pain is something distinct from heat, and the consequence or effect of it.

Phil.   Upon putting your hand near the fire, do you perceive one simple uniform sensation, or two distinct sensations?

Hyl.   But one simple sensation.

Phil.   Is not the heat immediately perceived?

Hyl.   It is.

Phil.   And the pain?

Hyl.   True.

Phil.   Seeing therefore they are both immediately perceived at the same time, and the fire affects you only with one simple or uncompounded idea, it follows that this same simple idea is both the intense heat immediately perceived, and the pain; and, consequently, that the intense heat immediately perceived is nothing distinct from a particular sort of pain.

Hyl.   It seems so.

Phil.   Again, try in your thoughts, Hylas, if you can conceive a vehement sensation to be without pain, or pleasure.

Hyl.   I cannot.

Phil.   Or can you frame to yourself an idea of sensible pain or pleasure in general, abstracted from every particular idea of heat, cold, tastes, smells? &c.

Hyl.   I do not find that I can.

Phil. Does it not therefore follow, that sensible pain is nothing distinct from those sensations or ideas, in an intense degree?

Hyl. It is undeniable; and, to speak the truth, I begin to suspect a very great heat cannot exist but in a mind perceiving it.

Phil. What! Are you then in that *skeptical* state of suspense, between affirming and denying?

Hyl. I think I may be positive in the point. A very violent and painful heat cannot exist without the mind.

Phil. It has not therefore, according to you, any real being.

Hyl. I own it.

Phil. Is it therefore certain, that there is no body in nature really hot?

Hyl. I have not denied there is any real heat in bodies. I only say, there is no such thing as an intense real heat.

Phil. But, did you not say before that all degrees of heat were equally real: or, if there was any difference, that the greater were more undoubtedly real than the lesser?

Hyl. True: but it was because I did not then consider the ground there is for distinguishing between them, which I now plainly see. And it is this: because intense heat is nothing else but a particular kind of painful sensation; and pain cannot exist but in a perceiving being; it follows that no intense heat can really exist in an unperceiving corporeal substance. But this is no reason why we should deny heat in an inferior degree to exist in such a substance.

Phil. But how shall we be able to discern those degrees of heat which exist only in the mind from those which exist without it?

Hyl. That is no difficult matter. You know the least pain cannot exist unperceived; whatever, therefore, degree of heat is a pain exists only in the mind. But as for all other degrees of heat, nothing obliges us to think the same of them.

Phil. I think you granted before that no unperceiving being was capable of pleasure, any more than of pain.

Hyl. I did.

Phil. And is not warmth, or a more gentle degree of heat than what causes uneasiness, a pleasure?

Hyl. What then?

Phil. Consequently, it cannot exist without the mind in an unperceiving substance, or body.

Hyl.   So it seems.

Phil.   Since therefore, as well those degrees of heat that are not painful, as those that are, can exist only in a thinking substance; may we not conclude that external bodies are absolutely incapable of any degree of heat whatsoever?

Hyl.   On second thought, I do not think it so evident that warmth is a pleasure as that a great degree of heat is a pain.

Phil.   I do not pretend that warmth is as great a pleasure as heat is a pain. But, if you grant it to be even a small pleasure, it serves to make good my conclusion.

Hyl.   I could rather call it an *indolence*. It seems to be nothing more than a privation of both pain and pleasure. And that such a quality or state as this may agree to an unthinking substance, I hope you will not deny.

Phil.   If you are resolved to maintain that warmth, or a gentle degree of heat, is no pleasure, I know not how to convince you otherwise, than by appealing to your own sense. But what think you of cold?

Hyl.   The same that I do of heat. An intense degree of cold is a pain; for to feel a very great cold, is to perceive a great uneasiness: it cannot therefore exist without the mind; but a lesser degree of cold may, as well as a lesser degree of heat.

Phil.   Those bodies, therefore, upon whose application to our own, we perceive a moderate degree of heat, must be concluded to have a moderate degree of heat or warmth in them: and those, upon whose application we feel a like degree of cold, must be thought to have cold in them.

Hyl.   They must.

Phil.   Can any doctrine be true that necessarily leads a man into an absurdity?

Hyl.   Without doubt it cannot.

Phil.   Is it not an absurdity to think that the same thing should be at the same time both cold and warm?

Hyl.   It is.

Phil.   Suppose now one of your hands hot, and the other cold, and that they are both at once put into the same vessel of water, in an intermediate state; will not the water seem cold to one hand, and warm to the other?

Hyl.   It will.

Phil. Ought we not therefore by your principles, to conclude it is really both cold and warm at the same time, that is, according to your own concession, to believe an absurdity?

Hyl. I confess it seems so.

Phil. Consequently, the principles themselves are false, since you have granted that no true principle leads to an absurdity.

Hyl. But after all, can anything be more absurd than to say, *there is no heat in the fire?*

Phil. To make the point still clearer; tell me, whether in two cases exactly alike, we ought not to make the same judgment?

Hyl. We ought.

Phil. When a pin pricks your finger, does it not rend and divide the fibres of your flesh?

Hyl. It does.

Phil. And when a coal burns your finger, does it any more?

Hyl. It does not.

Phil. Since therefore, you neither judge the sensation itself occasioned by the pin, nor anything like it to be in the pin; you should not, conformably to what you have now granted, judge the sensation occasioned by the fire, or anything like it, to be in the fire.

Hyl. Well, since it must be so, I am content to yield this point, and acknowledge, that heat and cold are only sensations existing in our minds: but there still remain qualities enough to secure the reality of external things.

Phil. But what will you say, Hylas, if it shall appear that the case is the same with regard to all other sensible qualities, and that they can no more be supposed to exist without the mind, than heat and cold?

Hyl. Then indeed you will have done something to the purpose; but that is what I despair of seeing proved.

Phil. Let us examine them in order. What think you of tastes, do they exist without the mind, or no?

Hyl. Can any man in his senses doubt whether sugar is sweet, or wormwood bitter?

Phil. Inform me, Hylas. Is a sweet taste a particular kind of pleasure or pleasant sensation, or is it not?

Hyl. It is.

Phil. And is not bitterness some kind of uneasiness or pain?

Hyl. I grant it.

Phil. If therefore sugar and wormwood are unthinking corporeal substances existing without the mind, how can sweetness and bitterness, that is, pleasure and pain, agree to them?

Hyl. Hold, Philonous, I now see what it was deluded me all this time. You asked whether heat and cold, sweetness and bitterness, were not particular sorts of pleasure and pain; to which I answered simply, that they were. Whereas I should have thus distinguished: those qualities, as perceived by us, are pleasures or pains; but not as existing in the external objects. We must not therefore conclude absolutely, that there is no heat in the fire, or sweetness in the sugar, but only that heat or sweetness, as perceived by us, are not in the fire or sugar. What say you to this?

Phil. I say it is nothing to the purpose. Our discourse proceeded altogether concerning sensible things, which you defined to be, the things we *immediately perceive by our senses*. Whatever other qualities therefore you speak of, as distinct from these, I know nothing of them, neither do they at all belong to the point in dispute. You may indeed pretend to have discovered certain qualities which you do not perceive, and assert those insensible qualities exist in fire and sugar. But what use can be made of this to your present purpose, I am at a loss to conceive. Tell me then once more, do you acknowledge that heat and cold, sweetness and bitterness (meaning those qualities which are perceived by the senses) do not exist without the mind?

Hyl. I see it is to no purpose to hold out, so I give up the cause as to those mentioned qualities. Though I profess it sounds oddly, to say that sugar is not sweet.

Phil. But for your farther satisfaction, take this along with you: that which at other times seems sweet, shall to a distempered palate appear bitter. And nothing can be plainer than that divers persons perceive different tastes in the same food, since that which one man delights in, another abhors. And how could this be, if the taste was something really inherent in the food?

Hyl. I acknowledge I know not how.

Phil. In the next place, odors are to be considered. And with regard to these, I would fain know whether what has been said of tastes does not exactly agree to them? Are they not so many pleasing or displeasing sensations?

Hyl. They are.

Phil.   Can you then conceive it possible that they should exist in an unperceiving thing?

Hyl.   I cannot.

Phil.   Or can you imagine that filth and ordure affect those brute animals that feed on them out of choice, with the same smells which we perceive in them?

Hyl.   By no means.

Phil.   May we not therefore conclude of smells, as of the other forementioned qualities, that they cannot exist in any but a perceiving substance or mind?

Hyl.   I think so.

Phil.   Then as to sounds, what must we think of them: are they accidents really inherent in external bodies, or not?

Hyl.   That they inhere not in the sonorous bodies is plain from hence: because a bell struck in the exhausted receiver of an air-pump sends forth no sound. The air therefore must be thought the subject of sound.

Phil.   What reason is there for that, Hylas?

Hyl.   Because when any motion is raised in the air, we perceive a sound greater or lesser, according to the air's motion; but without some motion in the air, we never hear any sound at all.

Phil.   And granting that we never hear a sound but when some motion is produced in the air, yet I do not see how you can infer from thence, that the sound itself is in the air.

Hyl.   It is this very motion in the external air, that produces in the mind the sensation of *sound*. For, striking on the drum of the ear, it causes a vibration, which by the auditory nerves being communicated to the brain, the soul is thereupon affected with the sensation called *sound*.

Phil.   What! Is sound then a sensation?

Hyl.   I tell you, as perceived by us, it is a particular sensation in the mind.

Phil.   And can any sensation exist without the mind?

Hyl.   No certainly.

Phil.   How then can sound, being a sensation, exist in the air, if by the *air* you mean a senseless substance existing without the mind?

Hyl.   You must distinguish, Philonous, between sound as it is perceived by us, and as it is in itself; or (which is the same thing) between the sound we immediately perceive, and that which exists without us. The former indeed is a particular kind of sensation, but the latter is merely a vibrative or undulatory motion in the air.

Phil. I thought I had already obviated that distinction by the answer I gave when you were applying it in a like case before. But to say no more of that; are you sure then that sound is really nothing but motion?

Hyl. I am.

Phil. Whatever therefore agrees to real sound, may with truth be attributed to motion?

Hyl. It may.

Phil. It is then good sense to speak of *motion*, as of a thing that is *loud, sweet, acute,* or *grave.*

Hyl. I see you are resolved not to understand me. Is it not evident, those accidents or modes belong only to sensible sound, or *sound* in the common acceptation of the word, but not to *sound* in the real and philosophic sense, which, as I just now told you, is nothing but a certain motion of the air?

Phil. It seems then there are two sorts of sound, the one vulgar, or that which is heard, the other philosophical and real?

Hyl. Even so.

Phil. And the latter consists in motion?

Hyl. I told you so before.

Phil. Tell me, Hylas, to which of the senses think you, the idea of motion belongs: to the hearing?

Hyl. No certainly, but to the sight and touch.

Phil. It should follow then, that according to you, real sounds may possibly be *seen* or *felt*, but never *heard*.

Hyl. Look you, Philonous, you may if you please make a jest of my opinion, but that will not alter the truth of things. I own indeed, the inferences you draw me into sound something oddly; but common language, you know, is framed by, and for the use of the vulgar: we must not therefore wonder, if expressions adapted to exact philosophic notions seem uncouth and out of the way.

Phil. Is it come to that? I assure you, I imagine myself to have gained no small point, since you make so light of departing from common phrases and opinion; it being a main part of our inquiry, to examine whose notions are widest of the common road, and most repugnant to the general sense of the world. But can you think it no more than a philosophical paradox, to say that *real sounds are never heard*, and that the idea of them is obtained by some other sense? And is there nothing in this contrary to nature and the truth of things?

Hyl. To deal ingenuously, I do not like it. And after the concessions already made, I had as well grant that sounds too have no real being without the mind.

Phil. And I hope you will make no difficulty to acknowledge the same of colors.

Hyl. Pardon me: the case of colors is very different. Can anything be plainer than that we see them on the objects?

Phil. The objects you speak of are, I suppose, corporeal substances existing without the mind?

Hyl. They are.

Phil. And have true and real colors inhering in them?

Hyl. Each visible object has that color which we see in it.

Phil. How! Is there anything visible but what we perceive by sight?

Hyl. There is not.

Phil. And do we perceive anything by sense which we do not perceive immediately?

Hyl. How often must I be obliged to repeat the same thing? I tell you, we do not.

Phil. Have patience, good Hylas; and tell me once more, whether there is anything immediately perceived by the senses, except sensible qualities. I know you asserted there was not: but I would now be informed, whether you still persist in the same opinion.

Hyl. I do.

Phil. Pray, is your corporeal substance either a sensible quality, or made up of sensible qualities?

Hyl. What a question that is! Who ever thought it was?

Phil. My reason for asking was, because in saying, *each visible object has that color which we see in it,* you make visible objects to be corporeal substances; which implies either that corporeal substances are sensible qualities, or else that there is something beside sensible qualities perceived by sight: but as this point was formerly agreed between us, and is still maintained by you, it is a clear consequence, that your corporeal substance is nothing distinct from sensible qualities.

Hyl. You may draw as many absurd consequences as you please, and endeavor to perplex the plainest things; but you shall never persuade me out of my senses. I clearly understand my own meaning.

Phil. I wish you would make me understand it too. But since you are unwilling to have your notion of corporeal substance examined, I shall urge that point no farther. Only be pleased to let me know, whether the same colors which we see exist in external bodies, or some other.

Hyl. The very same.

Phil. What! Are then the beautiful red and purple we see on yonder clouds really in them? Or do you imagine they have in themselves any other form, than that of a dark mist or vapor?

Hyl. I must own, Philonous, those colors are not really in the clouds as they seem to be at this distance. They are only apparent colors.

Phil. *Apparent* call you them? How shall we distinguish these apparent colors from real?

Hyl. Very easily. Those are to be thought apparent, which appearing only at a distance, vanish upon a nearer approach.

Phil. And those I suppose are to be thought real, which are discovered by the most near and exact survey.

Hyl. Right.

Phil. Is the nearest and exactest survey made by the help of a microscope, or by the naked eye?

Hyl. By a microscope, doubtless.

Phil. But a microscope often discovers colors in an object different from those perceived by the unassisted sight. And in case we had microscopes magnifying to any assigned degree; it is certain that no object whatsoever viewed through them, would appear in the same color which it exhibits to the naked eye.

Hyl. And what will you conclude from all this? You cannot argue that there are really and naturally no colors on objects: because by artificial managements they may be altered, or made to vanish.

Phil. I think it may evidently be concluded from your own concessions, that all the colors we see with our naked eyes, are only apparent as those on the clouds, since they vanish upon a more close and accurate inspection which is afforded us by a microscope. Then as to what you say by way of prevention: I ask you, whether the real and natural state of an object is better discovered by a very sharp and piercing sight, or by one which is less sharp?

Hyl.   By the former without doubt.

Phil.   Is it not plain from *dioptrics* that microscopes make the sight more penetrating, and represent objects as they would appear to the eye, in case it were naturally endowed with a most exquisite sharpness?

Hyl.   It is.

Phil.   Consequently the microscopical representation is to be thought that which best sets forth the real nature of the thing, or what it is in itself. The colors therefore by it perceived, are more genuine and real than those perceived otherwise.

Hyl.   I confess there is something in what you say.

Phil.   Besides, it is not only possible but manifest, that there actually are animals, whose eyes are by nature framed to perceive those things, which by reason of their minuteness escape our sight. What think you of those inconceivably small animals perceived by glasses? Must we suppose they are all stark blind? Or, in case they see, can it be imagined their sight has not the same use in preserving their bodies from injuries, which appears in that of all other animals? And if it has, is it not evident, they must see particles less than their own bodies, which will present them with a far different view in each object from that which strikes our senses? Even our own eyes do not always represent objects to us after the same manner. In the *jaundice*, every one knows that all things seem yellow. Is it not therefore highly probable, those animals in whose eyes we discern a very different texture from that of ours, and whose bodies abound with different humors, do not see the same colors in every object that we do? From all which, should it not seem to follow, that all colors are equally apparent, and that none of those which we perceive are really inherent in any outward object?

Hyl.   It should.

Phil.   The point will be past all doubt, if you consider, that in case colors were real properties or affections inherent in external bodies, they could admit of no alteration, without some change wrought in the very bodies themselves: but is it not evident from what has been said, that upon the use of microscopes, upon a change happening in the humors of the eye, or a variation of distance, without any manner of real alteration in the thing itself, the colors of any object are either changed, or totally disappear? Nay, all other circumstances remaining the same, change but the situation of some objects, and they shall present different colors to the eye. The same thing happens upon viewing an object in various degrees of light. And what is more known than that the same bodies appear differently colored by candle-light, from what they do in the open day? Add to these the experiment of a prism, which separating the heterogeneous rays of light, alters the color of any object; and will cause the whitest to appear of a deep blue or red to the naked eye. And now tell me whether you are still of opinion, that every body has its true real color inhering in it; and, if you think it has, I would fain know farther from you, what certain distance and position of the object, what peculiar texture and formation of the eye, what degree or kind of light is necessary for ascertaining that true color, and distinguishing it from apparent ones.

Hyl. I own myself entirely satisfied, that they are all equally apparent; and that there is no such thing as color really inhering in external bodies, but that it is altogether in the light. And what confirms me in this opinion is, that in proportion to the light, colors are still more or less vivid; and if there be no light, then are there no colors perceived. Besides, allowing there are colors on external objects, yet how is it possible for us to perceive them? For no external body affects the mind, unless it acts first on our organs of sense. But the only action of bodies is motion; and motion cannot be communicated otherwise than by impulse. A distant object therefore cannot act on the eye, nor consequently make itself or its properties perceivable to the soul. Whence it plainly follows that it is immediately some contiguous substance, which operating on the eye occasions a perception of colors: and such is light.

Phil. How! Is light then a substance?

Hyl. I tell you, Philonous, external light is nothing but a thin fluid substance, whose minute particles being agitated with a brisk motion, and in various manners reflected from the different surfaces of outward objects to the eyes, communicate different motions to the optic nerves; which being propagated to the brain, cause therein various impressions: and these are attended with the sensations of red, blue, yellow, &c.

Phil. It seems then the light does no more than shake the optic nerves.

Hyl. Nothing else.

Phil. And consequent to each particular motion of the nerves the mind is affected with a sensation, which is some particular color.

Hyl. Right.

Phil. And these sensations have no existence without the mind.

Hyl. They have not.

Phil.   How then do you affirm that colors are in the light, since by *light* you understand a corporeal substance external to the mind?

Hyl.   Light and colors, as immediately perceived by us, I grant cannot exist without the mind. But in themselves they are only the motions and configurations of certain insensible particles of matter.

Phil.   Colors then in the vulgar sense, or taken for the immediate objects of sight, cannot agree to any but a perceiving substance.

Hyl.   That is what I say.

Phil.   Well then, since you give up the point as to those sensible qualities, which are alone thought colors by all mankind beside, you may hold what you please with regard to those invisible ones of the philosophers. It is not my business to dispute about them; only I would advise you to bethink yourself, whether considering the inquiry we are upon, it be prudent for you to affirm, *the red and blue which we see are not real colors, but certain unknown motions and figures which no man ever did or can see, are truly so.* Are these not shocking notions, and are not they subject to as many ridiculous inferences, as those you were obliged to renounce before in the case of sounds?

Hyl.   I frankly own, Philonous, that it is in vain to stand out any longer. Colors, sounds, tastes, in a word, all those termed *secondary qualities*, have certainly no existence without the mind. But by this acknowledgment I must not be supposed to derogate anything from the reality of matter, or external objects, seeing it is no more than several philosophers maintain, who nevertheless are the farthest imaginable from denying matter. For the clearer understanding of this, you must know sensible qualities are by philosophers divided into *primary* and *secondary*. The former are extension, figure, solidity, gravity, motion, and rest. And these they hold exist really in bodies. The latter are those above enumerated; or briefly, all sensible qualities beside the primary, which they assert are only so many sensations or ideas existing nowhere but in the mind. But all this, I doubt not, you are apprised of. For my part, I have been a long time sensible there was such an opinion current among philosophers, but was never thoroughly convinced of its truth until now.

Phil.   You are still then of the opinion, that extension and figures are inherent in external unthinking substances?

Hyl.   I am.

Phil.   But what if the same arguments which are brought against secondary qualities, will hold good against these also?

Hyl. Why then I shall be obliged to think, they too exist only in the mind.

Phil. Is it your opinion, the very figure and extension which you perceive by sense exist in the outward object or material substance?

Hyl. It is.

Phil. Have all other animals as good grounds to think the same of the figure and extension which they see and feel?

Hyl. Without doubt, if they have any thought at all.

Phil. Answer me, Hylas. Think you the senses were bestowed upon all animals for their preservation and well-being in life? Or were they given to men alone for this end?

Hyl. I make no question but they have the same use in all other animals.

Phil. If so, is it not necessary they should be enabled by them to perceive their own limbs, and those bodies which are capable of harming them?

Hyl. Certainly.

Phil. A mite therefore must be supposed to see his own foot, and things equal or even less than it, as bodies of some considerable dimension; though at the same time they appear to you scarce discernible, or at best as so many visible points?

Hyl. I cannot deny it.

Phil. And to creatures less than the mite they will seem yet larger?

Hyl. They will.

Phil. Insomuch that what you can hardly discern, will to another extremely minute animal appear as some huge mountain?

Hyl. All this I grant.

Phil. Can one and the same thing be at the same time in itself of different dimensions?

Hyl. That were absurd to imagine.

Phil. But from what you have laid down it follows, that both the extension by you perceived, and that perceived by the mite itself, as likewise all those perceived by lesser animals, are each of them the true extension of the mite's foot, that is to say, by your own principles you are led into an absurdity.

Hyl. There seems to be some difficulty in the point.

Phil. Again, have you not acknowledged that no real inherent property of any object can be changed without some change in the thing itself?

Hyl. I have.

Phil. But, as we approach to or recede from an object, the visible extension varies, being at one distance ten or a hundred times greater than at another. Does it not therefore follow from hence likewise, that it is not really inherent in the object?

Hyl. I own that I am at a loss what to think.

Phil. Your judgment will soon be determined, if you will venture to think as freely concerning this quality, as you have done concerning the rest. Was it not admitted as a good argument, that neither heat nor cold was in the water, because it seemed warm to one hand and cold to the other?

Hyl. It was.

Phil. Is it not the very same reasoning to conclude, there is no extension or figure in an object, because to one eye it shall seem little, smooth, and round, when at the same time it appears to the other, great, uneven, and angular?

Hyl. The very same. But does this latter fact ever happen?

Phil. You may at any time make the experiment, by looking with one eye bare, and with the other through a microscope.

Hyl. I know not how to maintain it, and yet I am loath to give up *extension*, I see so many odd consequences following upon such a concession.

Phil. Odd, you say? After the concessions already made, I hope you will stick at nothing for its oddness. [But on the other hand should it not seem very odd, if the general reasoning which includes all other sensible qualities did not also include extension? If it be allowed that no idea nor anything like an idea can exist in an unperceiving substance, then surely it follows that no figure or mode of extension, which we can either perceive or imagine, or have any idea of, can be really inherent in matter; not to mention the peculiar difficulty there must be, in conceiving a material substance, prior to and distinct from extension, to be the *substratum* of extension. Be the sensible quality what it will, figure, or sound, or color; it seems impossible it should subsist in that which does not perceive it.]*

---

* Added in the third edition.

Hyl.   I give up the point for the present, reserving still a right to retract my opinion, in case I shall hereafter discover any false step in my progress to it.

Phil.   That is a right you cannot be denied. Figures and extension being dispatched, we proceed next to *motion*. Can a real motion in any external body be at the same time both very swift and very slow?

Hyl.   It cannot.

Phil.   Is not the motion of a body swift in a reciprocal proportion to the time it takes up in describing any given space? Thus a body that describes a mile in an hour, moves three times faster than it would in case it described only a mile in three hours.

Hyl.   I agree with you.

Phil.   And is not time measured by the succession of ideas in our minds?

Hyl.   It is.

Phil.   And is it not possible ideas should succeed one another twice as fast in your mind, as they do in mine, or in that of some spirit of another kind?

Hyl.   I own it.

Phil.   Consequently the same body may to another seem to perform its motion over any space in half the time that it does to you. And the same reasoning will hold as to any proportion: that is to say, according to your principles (since the motions perceived are both really in the object) it is possible one and the same body shall be really moved the same way at once, both very swift and very slow. How is this consistent either with common sense, or with what you just now granted?

Hyl.   I have nothing to say to it.

Phil.   Then as for *solidity*; either you do not mean any sensible quality by that word, and so it is beside our inquiry: or if you do, it must be either hardness or resistance. But both the one and the other are plainly relative to our senses: it being evident that what seems hard to one animal may appear soft to another, who has greater force and firmness of limbs. Nor is it less plain, that the resistance I feel is not in the body.

Hyl.   I own the very sensation of resistance, which is all you immediately perceive, is not in the *body*, but the cause of that sensation is.

Phil.   But the causes of our sensations are not things immediately perceived, and therefore are not sensible. This point I thought had been already determined.

Hyl. I own it was; but you will pardon me if I seem a little embarrassed: I know not how to quit my old notions.

Phil. To help you out, do but consider, that if extension be once acknowledged to have no existence without the mind, the same must necessarily be granted of motion, solidity, and gravity since they all evidently suppose extension. It is therefore superfluous to inquire particularly concerning each of them. In denying extension, you have denied them all to have any real existence.

Hyl. I wonder, Philonous, if what you say be true, why those philosophers who deny the secondary qualities any real existence, should yet attribute it to the primary. If there is no difference between them, how can this be accounted for?

Phil. It is not my business to account for every opinion of the philosophers. But among other reasons which may be assigned for this, it seems probable, that pleasure and pain being rather annexed to the former than the latter, may be one. Heat and cold, tastes and smells, have something more vividly pleasing or disagreeable than the ideas of extension, figure, and motion affect us with. And it being too visibly absurd to hold, that pain or pleasure can be in an unperceiving substance, men are more easily weaned from believing the external existence of the secondary, than the primary qualities. You will be satisfied there is something in this, if you recollect the difference you made between an intense and more moderate degree of heat, allowing the one a real existence, while you denied it to the other. But after all, there is no rational ground for that distinction; for surely an indifferent sensation is as truly *a sensation*, as one more pleasing or painful; and consequently should not any more than they be supposed to exist in an unthinking subject.

Hyl. It is just come into my head, Philonous, that I have somewhere heard of a distinction between absolute and sensible extension. Now though it be acknowledged that *great* and *small*, consisting merely in the relation which other extended beings have to the parts of our own bodies, do not really inhere in the substances themselves; yet nothing obliges us to hold the same with regard to *absolute extension*, which is something abstracted from *great* and *small*, from this or that particular magnitude or figure. So likewise as to motion, *swift* and *slow* are altogether relative to the succession of ideas in our own minds. But it does not follow, because those modifications of motion exist not without the mind, that therefore absolute motion abstracted from them does not.

Phil.   Pray what is it that distinguishes one motion, or one part of extension, from another? Is it not something sensible, as some degree of swiftness or slowness, some certain magnitude or figure peculiar to each?

Hyl.   I think so.

Phil.   These qualities therefore stripped of all sensible properties, are without all specific and numerical differences, as the schools call them.

Hyl.   They are.

Phil.   That is to say, they are extension in general, and motion in general.

Hyl.   Let it be so.

Phil.   But it is a universally received maxim that *everything which exists is particular.* How then can motion in general, or extension in general exist in any corporeal substance?

Hyl.   I will take time to solve your difficulty.

Phil.   But I think the point may be speedily decided. Without doubt you can tell, whether you are able to frame this or that idea. Now I am content to put our dispute on this issue. If you can frame in your thoughts a distinct abstract idea of motion or extension, divested of all those sensible modes, as swift and slow, great and small, round and square, and the like, which are acknowledged to exist only in the mind, I will then yield the point you contend for. But if you cannot, it will be unreasonable on your side to insist any longer upon what you have no notion of.

Hyl.   To confess ingenuously, I cannot.

Phil.   Can you even separate the ideas of extension and motion, from the ideas of all those qualities which they who make the distinction, term *secondary*?

Hyl.   What! Is it not an easy matter, to consider extension and motion by themselves, abstracted from all other sensible qualities? Pray how do the mathematicians treat of them?

Phil.   I acknowledge, Hylas, it is not difficult to form general propositions and reasonings about those qualities, without mentioning any other; and in this sense, to consider or treat of them abstractedly. But how does it follow that because I can pronounce the word *motion* by itself, I can form the idea of it in my mind exclusive of body? Or because theorems may be made of extension and figures, without any mention of *great* or *small*, or any other sensible mode or quality; that therefore it is possible such an abstract idea of extension, without any particular size or figure, or sensible quality, should be distinctly formed, and apprehended by the mind? Mathematicians treat of quantity, without regarding what other sensible qualities it is attended with, as being altogether indifferent to their demonstrations. But when laying aside the words, they contemplate the bare ideas, I believe you will find, they are not the pure abstracted ideas of extension.

Hyl. But what say you to *pure intellect*? May not abstracted ideas be framed by that faculty?

Phil. Since I cannot frame abstract ideas at all, it is plain, I cannot frame them by the help of *pure intellect*, whatsoever faculty you understand by those words. Besides, not to inquire into the nature of pure intellect and its spiritual objects, as *virtue, reason, God*, or the like; thus much seems manifest, that sensible things are only to be perceived by sense, or represented by the imagination. Figures therefore and extension being originally perceived by sense, do not belong to pure intellect. But for your farther satisfaction, try if you can frame the idea of any figure, abstracted from all particularities of size, or even from other sensible qualities.

Hyl. Let me think a little — I do not find that I can.

Phil. And can you think it possible, that should really exist in nature, which implies a repugnancy in its conception?

Hyl. By no means.

Phil. Since therefore it is impossible even for the mind to disunite the ideas of extension and motion from all other sensible qualities, does it not follow, that where the one exist, there necessarily the other exist likewise?

Hyl. It should seem so.

Phil. Consequently the very same arguments which you admitted, as conclusive against the secondary qualities, are without any farther application of force against the primary too. Besides, if you will trust your senses, is it not plain all sensible qualities coexist, or to them, appear as being in the same place? Do they ever represent a motion, or figure, as being divested of all other visible and tangible qualities?

Hyl. You need say no more on this head. I am free to own, if there be no secret error or oversight in our proceedings hitherto, that all sensible qualities are alike to be denied existence without the mind. But my fear is, that I have been too liberal in my former concessions, or overlooked some fallacy or other. In short, I did not take time to think.

Phil. For that matter, Hylas, you may take what time you please in reviewing the progress of our inquiry. You are at liberty to recover any slips you might have made, or offer whatever you have omitted, which makes for your first opinion.

Hyl. One great oversight I take to be this: that I did not sufficiently distinguish the *object* from the *sensation*. Now though this latter may not exist without the mind, yet it will not thence follow that the former cannot.

Phil. What object do you mean? The object of the senses?

Hyl. The same.

Phil. It is then immediately perceived?

Hyl. Right.

Phil. Make me to understand the difference between what is immediately perceived, and a sensation.

Hyl. The sensation I take to be an act of the mind perceiving; beside which, there is something perceived; and this I call the *object*. For example, there is red and yellow on that tulip. But then the act of perceiving those colors is in me only, and not in the tulip.

Phil. What tulip do you speak of? Is it that which you see?

Hyl. The same.

Phil. And what do you see beside color, figure, and extension?

Hyl. Nothing.

Phil. What you would say then is, that the red and yellow are coexistent with the extension; is it not?

Hyl. That is not all; I would say, they have a real existence without the mind, in some unthinking substance.

Phil. That the colors are really in the tulip which I see, is manifest. Neither can it be denied, that this tulip may exist independent of your mind or mine; but that any immediate object of the senses, that is, any idea, or combination of ideas, should exist in an unthinking substance, or exterior to all minds, is in itself an evident contradiction. Nor can I imagine how this follows from what you said just now, to wit that the red and yellow were on the tulip *you saw*, since you do not pretend to see that unthinking substance.

Hyl. You have an artful way, Philonous, of diverting our inquiry from the subject.

Phil. I see you have no mind to be pressed that way. To return then to your distinction between *sensation* and *object*; if I take you right, you distinguish in every perception two things, the one an action of the mind, the other not.

Hyl.　True.

Phil.　And this action cannot exist in, or belong to any unthinking thing; but whatever beside is implied in a perception, may?

Hyl.　That is my meaning.

Phil.　So that if there was a perception without any act of the mind, it were possible such a perception should exist in an unthinking substance?

Hyl.　I grant it. But it is impossible there should be such a perception.

Phil.　When is the mind said to be active?

Hyl.　When it produces, puts an end to, or changes, anything.

Phil.　Can the mind produce, discontinue, or change anything but by an act of the will?

Hyl.　It cannot.

Phil.　The mind therefore is to be accounted active in its perceptions, so far forth as volition is included in them?

Hyl.　It is.

Phil.　In plucking this flower, I am active, because I do it by the motion of my hand, which was consequent upon my volition; so likewise in applying it to my nose. But is either of these smelling?

Hyl.　No.

Phil.　I act too in drawing the air through my nose; because my breathing so rather than otherwise, is the effect of my volition. But neither can this be called *smelling*: for if it were, I should smell every time I breathed in that manner?

Hyl.　True.

Phil.　Smelling then is somewhat consequent to all this?

Hyl.　It is.

Phil.　But I do not find my will concerned any farther. Whatever more there is, as that I perceive such a particular smell or any smell at all, this is independent of my will, and therein I am altogether passive. Do you find it otherwise with you, Hylas?

Hyl.　No, the very same.

Phil.　Then as to seeing, is it not in your power to open your eyes, or keep them shut; to turn them this or that way?

Hyl.　Without doubt.

Phil. But does it in like manner depend on your will, that in looking on this flower you perceive *white* rather than any other color? Or directing your open eyes towards yonder part of the heaven, can you avoid seeing the sun? Or is light or darkness the effect of your volition?

Hyl. No certainly.

Phil. Your are then in these respects altogether passive?

Hyl. I am.

Phil. Tell me now, whether *seeing* consists in perceiving light and colors, or in opening and turning the eyes?

Hyl. Without doubt, in the former.

Phil. Since therefore you are in the very perception of light and colors altogether passive, what is become of that action you were speaking of, as an ingredient in every sensation? And does it not follow from your own concessions, that the perception of light and colors, including no action in it, may exist in an unperceiving substance? And is not this a plain contradiction?

Hyl. I know not what to think of it.

Phil. Besides, since you distinguish the *active* and *passive* in every perception, you must do it in that of pain. But how is it possible that pain, be it as little active as you please, should exist in an unperceiving substance? In short, do but consider the point, and then confess ingenuously, whether light and colors, tastes, sounds, &c. are not all equally passions or sensations in the soul. You may indeed call them *external objects*, and give them in words what subsistence you please. But examine your own thoughts, and then tell me whether it be not as I say?

Hyl. I acknowledge, Philonous, that, upon a fair observation of what passes in my mind, I can discover nothing else, but that I am a thinking being, affected with variety of sensations; neither is it possible to conceive how a sensation should exist in an unperceiving substance. But then on the other hand, when I look on sensible things in a different view, considering them as so many modes and qualities, I find it necessary to suppose a material *substratum*, without which they cannot be conceived to exist.

Phil. *Material substratum* call you it? Pray, by which of your senses came you acquainted with that being?

Hyl. It is not itself sensible; its modes and qualities only being perceived by the senses.

Phil. I presume then it was by reflection and reason you obtained the idea of it?

Hyl. I do not pretend to any proper positive idea of it. However I conclude it exists, because qualities cannot be conceived to exist without a support.

Phil. It seems then you have only a relative notion of it, or that you conceive it not otherwise than by conceiving the relation it bears to sensible qualities?

Hyl. Right.

Phil. Be pleased therefore to let me know wherein that relation consists.

Hyl. Is it not sufficiently expressed in the term *substratum*, or *substance*?

Phil. If so, the word *substratum* should import, that it is spread under the sensible qualities or accidents?

Hyl. True.

Phil. And consequently under extension?

Hyl. I own it.

Phil. It is therefore somewhat in its own nature entirely distinct from extension?

Hyl. I tell you, extension is only a mode, and matter is something that supports modes. And is it not evident the thing supported is different from the thing supporting?

Phil. So that something distinct from, and exclusive of, extension is supposed to be the *substratum* of extension?

Hyl. Just so.

Phil. Answer me, Hylas. Can a thing be spread without extension? Or is not the idea of extension necessarily included in *spreading*?

Hyl. It is.

Phil. Whatsoever therefore you suppose spread under anything, must have in itself an extension distinct from the extension of that thing under which it is spread?

Hyl. It must.

Phil. Consequently every corporeal substance being the *substratum* of extension, must have in itself another extension by which it is qualified to be a *substratum*: and so on to infinity? And I ask whether this be not absurd in itself, and repugnant to what you granted just now, to wit, that the *substratum* was something distinct from and exclusive of extension?

Hyl. Aye but, Philonous, you take me wrong. I do not mean that matter is spread in a gross literal sense under extension. The word substratum is used only to express in general the same thing with *substance*.

Phil. Well then, let us examine the relation implied in the term *substance*. Is it not that it stands under accidents?

Hyl. The very same.

Phil. But, that one thing may stand under or support another, must it not be extended?

Hyl. It must.

Phil. Is not therefore this supposition liable to the same absurdity with the former?

Hyl. You still take things in a strict literal sense. That is not fair, Philonous.

Phil. I am not for imposing any sense on your words: you are at liberty to explain them as you please. Only, I beseech you, make me understand something by them. You tell me matter supports or stands under accidents. How? Is it as your legs support your body?

Hyl. No; that is the literal sense.

Phil. Pray let me know any sense, literal or not literal, that you understand it in. — How long must I wait for an answer, Hylas?

Hyl. I declare I know not what to say. I once thought I understood well enough what was meant by matter's supporting accidents. But now, the more I think on it the less can I comprehend it: in short I find that I know nothing of it.

Phil. It seems then you have no idea at all, neither relative nor positive, of matter; you know neither what it is in itself, nor what relation it bears to accidents?

Hyl. I acknowledge it.

Phil. And yet you asserted that you could not conceive how qualities or accidents should really exist, without conceiving at the same time a material support of them?

Hyl. I did.

Phil. That is to say, when you conceive the real existence of qualities, you do withal conceive Something which you cannot conceive?

Hyl. It was wrong, I own. But still I fear there is some fallacy or other. Pray what think you of this? It is just come into my head that the ground of all our mistakes lies in your treating of each quality by itself. Now, I grant that each quality cannot singly subsist without the mind. Color cannot without extension, neither can figure without some other sensible quality. But, as the several qualities united or blended together form entire sensible things, nothing hinders why such things may not be supposed to exist without the mind.

Phil. Either, Hylas, you are jesting, or have a very bad memory. Though indeed we went through all the qualities by name one after another, yet my arguments, or rather your concessions, nowhere tended to prove that the secondary qualities did not subsist each alone by itself; but, that they were not at all without the mind. Indeed, in treating of figure and motion we concluded they could not exist without the mind, because it was impossible even in thought to separate them from all secondary qualities, so as to conceive them existing by themselves. But then this was not the only argument made use of upon that occasion. But (to pass by all that has been hitherto said, and reckon it for nothing, if you will have it so) I am content to put the whole upon this issue. If you can conceive it possible for any mixture or combination of qualities, or any sensible object whatever, to exist without the mind, then I will grant it actually to be so.

Hyl. If it comes to that the point will soon be decided. What more easy than to conceive a tree or house existing by itself, independent of, and unperceived by, any mind whatsoever? I do at this present time conceive them existing after that manner.

Phil. How say you, Hylas, can you see a thing which is at the same time unseen?

Hyl. No, that were a contradiction.

Phil. Is it not as great a contradiction to talk of conceiving a thing which is unconceived?

Hyl. It is.

Phil. The tree or house therefore which you think of is conceived by you?

Hyl. How should it be otherwise?

Phil. And what is conceived is surely in the mind?

Hyl. Without question, that which is conceived is in the mind.

Phil. How then came you to say, you conceived a house or tree existing independent and out of all minds whatsoever?

Hyl. That was I own an oversight; but stay, let me consider what led me into it. — It is a pleasant mistake enough. As I was thinking of a tree in a solitary place, where no one was present to see it, methought that was to conceive a tree as existing unperceived or unthought of; not considering that I myself conceived it all the while. But now I plainly see that all I can do is to frame ideas in my own mind. I may indeed conceive in my own thoughts the idea of a tree, or a house, or a mountain, but that is all. And this is far from proving that I can conceive them existing out of the minds of all Spirits.

Phil. You acknowledge then that you cannot possibly conceive how any one corporeal sensible thing should exist otherwise than in a mind?

Hyl. I do.

Phil. And yet you will earnestly contend for the truth of that which you cannot so much as conceive?

Hyl. I profess I know not what to think; but still there are some scruples remain with me. Is it not certain I see things at a distance? Do we not perceive the stars and moon, for example, to be a great way off? Is not this, I say, manifest to the senses?

Phil. Do you not in a dream too perceive those or the like objects?

Hyl. I do.

Phil. And have they not then the same appearance of being distant?

Hyl. They have.

Phil. But you do not thence conclude the apparitions in a dream to be without the mind?

Hyl. By no means.

Phil. You ought not therefore to conclude that sensible objects are without the mind, from their appearance, or manner wherein they are perceived.

Hyl. I acknowledge it. But does not my sense deceive me in those cases?

Phil. By no means. The idea or thing which you immediately perceive, neither sense nor reason informs you that it actually exists without the mind. By sense you only know that you are affected with such certain sensations of light and colors, &c. And these you will not say are without the mind.

Hyl.   True: but, beside all that, do you not think the sight suggests something of outness or distance?

Phil.   Upon approaching a distant object, do the visible size and figure change perpetually, or do they appear the same at all distance?

Hyl.   They are in a continual change.

Phil.   Sight therefore does not suggest, or any way inform you, that the visible object you immediately perceive exists at a distance, or will be perceived when you advance further onward; there being a continued series of visible objects succeeding each other during the whole time of your approach.

Hyl.   It does not; but still I know, upon seeing an object, what object I shall perceive after having passed over a certain distance: no matter whether it be exactly the same or no: there is still something of distance suggested in the case.

Phil.   Good Hylas, do but reflect a little on the point, and then tell me whether there be any more in it than this: From the ideas you actually perceive by sight, you have by experience learned to collect what other ideas you will (according to the standing orders of nature) be affected with, after a certain succession of time and motion.

Hyl.   Upon the whole, I take it to be nothing else.

Phil.   Now, is it not plain that if we suppose a man blind was on a sudden made to see, he could at first have no experience of what may be suggested by sight?

Hyl.   It is.

Phil.   He would not then, according to you, have any notion of distance annexed to the things he saw; but would take them for a new set of sensations, existing in his mind?

Hyl.   It is undeniable.

Phil.   But, to make it still more plain: is not distance a line turned endwise to the eye?

Hyl.   It is.

Phil.   And can a line so situated be perceived by sight?

Hyl.   It cannot.

Phil.   Does it not therefore follow that distance is not properly and immediately perceived by sight?

Hyl.   It should seem so.

Phil.   Again, is it your opinion that colors are at a distance?

Hyl.   It must be acknowledged they are only in the mind.

Phil.   But do not colors appear to the mind as coexisting in the same place with extension and figures?

Hyl.   They do.

Phil.   How can you then conclude from sight that figures exist without, when you acknowledge colors do not; the sensible appearance being the very same with regard to both?

Hyl.   I know not what to answer.

Phil.   But, allowing that distance was truly and immediately perceived by the mind, yet it would not thence follow it existed out of the mind. For, whatever is immediately perceived is an idea: and can any idea exist out of the mind?

Hyl.   To suppose that were absurd: but, inform me, Philonous, can we perceive or know nothing besides our ideas?

Phil.   As for the rational deducing of causes from effects, that is beside our inquiry. And, by the senses you can best tell whether you perceive anything which is not immediately perceived. And I ask you, whether the things immediately perceived are other than your own sensations or ideas? You have indeed more than once, in the course of this conversation, declared yourself on these points; but you seem, by this last question, to have departed from what you then thought.

Hyl.   To speak the truth, Philonous, I think there are two kinds of objects: — the one perceived immediately, which are likewise called ideas; the other are real things or external objects, perceived by the mediation of ideas, which are their images and representations. Now, I own ideas do not exist outside the mind; but the latter sort of objects do. I am sorry I did not think of this distinction sooner; it would probably have cut short your discourse.

Phil.   Are those external objects perceived by sense, or by some other faculty?

Hyl.   They are perceived by sense.

Phil.   How! Is there anything perceived by sense that is not immediately perceived?

Hyl.   Yes, Philonous, in some sort there is. For example, when I look on a picture or statue of Julius Caesar, I may be said after a manner to perceive him (though not immediately) by my senses.

Phil.   It seems then you will have our ideas, which alone are immediately perceived, to be pictures of external things: and that these also are perceived by sense, inasmuch as they have a conformity or resemblance to our ideas?

Hyl.   That is my meaning.

Phil.   And, in the same way that Julius Caesar, in himself invisible, is nevertheless perceived by sight; real things, in themselves imperceptible, are perceived by sense.

Hyl.   In the very same.

Phil.   Tell me, Hylas, when you behold the picture of Julius Caesar, do you see with your eyes any more than some colors and figures, with a certain symmetry and composition of the whole?

Hyl.   Nothing else.

Phil.   And would not a man who had never known anything of Julius Caesar see as much?

Hyl.   He would.

Phil.   Consequently, he has his sight, and his use of it, in as perfect a degree as you?

Hyl.   I agree with you.

Phil.   Whence comes it then that your thoughts are directed to the Roman emperor, and his are not? This cannot proceed from the sensations or ideas of sense by you then perceived; since you acknowledge you have no advantage over him in that respect. It should seem therefore to proceed from reason and memory: should it not?

Hyl.   It should.

Phil.   Consequently, it will not follow from that instance that anything is perceived by sense which is not immediately perceived. Though I grant we may, in one acceptation, be said to perceive sensible things mediately by sense: that is, when, from a frequently perceived connection, the immediate perception of ideas by one sense suggests to the mind others, perhaps belonging to another sense, which are wont to be connected with them. For instance, when I hear a coach drive along the streets, immediately I perceive only the sound; but, from the experience I have had that such a sound is connected with a coach, I am said to hear the coach. It is nevertheless evident that, in truth and strictness, nothing can be heard but sound; and the coach is not then properly perceived by sense, but suggested from experience. So likewise when we are said to see a red-hot bar of iron; the solidity and heat of the iron are not the objects of sight, but suggested to the imagination by the color and figure which are properly perceived by sense. In short, those things alone are actually and strictly perceived by any sense, which would have been perceived in case that same sense had then been first conferred on us. As for other things, it is plain they are only suggested to the mind by experience, grounded on former perceptions. But, to return to your comparison of Caesar's picture, it is plain, if you keep to that, you must hold the real things, or archetypes of our ideas, are not perceived by sense, but by some internal faculty of the soul, as reason or memory. I would therefore fain know what arguments you can draw from reason for the existence of what you call real things or material objects. Or whether you remember to have seen them formerly as they are in themselves; or, if you have heard or read of any one that did.

Hyl. I see, Philonous, you are disposed to raillery; but that will never convince me.

Phil. My aim is only to learn from you the way to come at the knowledge of material beings. Whatever we perceive is perceived immediately or mediately: by sense or by reason and reflection. But, as you have excluded sense, pray show me what reason you have to believe their existence; or what medium you can possibly make use of to prove it, either to mine or to your own understanding.

Hyl. To deal ingenuously, Philonous, now I consider the point, I do not find I can give you any good reason for it. But, thus much seems pretty plain, that it is at least possible such things may really exist. And, as long as there is no absurdity in supposing them, I am resolved to believe as I did, till you bring good reasons to the contrary.

Phil. What! Is it come to this, that you only believe the existence of material objects, and that your belief is founded barely on the possibility of its being true? Then you will have me bring reasons against it: though another would think it reasonable the proof should lie on him who holds the affirmative. And, after all, this very point which you are now resolved to maintain, without any reason, is in effect what you have more than once during this discourse seen good reason to give up. But to pass over all this; if I understand you rightly, you say our ideas do not exist without the mind, but that they are copies, images, or representations, of certain originals that do?

Hyl. You take me right.

Phil. They are then like external things?

Hyl. They are.

Phil. Have those things a stable and permanent nature, independent of our senses; or are they in a perpetual change, upon our producing any motions in our bodies — suspending, exerting, or altering, our faculties or organs of sense?

Hyl. Real things, it is plain, have a fixed and real nature, which remains the same notwithstanding any change in our senses or in the posture and motion of our bodies; which indeed may affect the ideas in our minds, but it were absurd to think they had the same effect on things existing without the mind.

Phil. How then is it possible that things perpetually fleeting and variable as our ideas should be copies or images of anything fixed and constant? Or, in other words, since all sensible qualities, as size, figure, color, &c., that is, our ideas, are continually changing, upon every alteration in the distance, medium, or instruments of sensation; how can any determinate material objects be properly represented or painted forth by several distinct things, each of which is so different from and unlike the rest? Or, if you say it resembles some one only of our ideas, how shall we be able to distinguish the true copy from all the false ones?

Hyl. I profess, Philonous, I am at a loss. I know not what to say to this.

Phil. But neither is this all. Which are material objects in themselves — perceptible or imperceptible?

Hyl. Properly and immediately nothing can be perceived but ideas. All material things, therefore, are in themselves insensible, and to be perceived, only by our ideas.

Phil. Ideas then are sensible, and their archetypes or originals insensible?

Hyl. Right.

Phil. But how can that which is sensible be like that which is insensible? Can a real thing, in itself invisible, be like a color; or a real thing, which is not audible, be like a sound? In a word, can anything be like a sensation or idea, but another sensation or idea?

Hyl. I must own, I think not.

Phil. Is it possible there should be any doubt on the point? Do you not perfectly know your own ideas?

Hyl. I know them perfectly; since what I do not perceive or know can be no part of my idea.

Phil. Consider, therefore, and examine them, and then tell me if there be anything in them which can exist without the mind: or if you can conceive anything like them existing without the mind.

Hyl. Upon inquiry, I find it is impossible for me to conceive or understand how anything but an idea can be like an idea. And it is most evident that no idea can exist without the mind.

Phil. You are therefore, by your principles, forced to deny the reality of sensible things; since you made it to consist in an absolute existence exterior to the mind. That is to say, you are a downright *skeptic*. So I have gained my point, which was to show your principles led to skepticism.

Hyl. For the present I am, if not entirely convinced, at least silenced.

Phil. I would fain know what more you would require in order to a perfect conviction. Have you not had the liberty of explaining yourself all manner of ways? Were any little slips in discourse laid hold and insisted on? Or were you not allowed to retract or reinforce anything you had offered, as best served your purpose? Has not everything you could say been heard and examined with all the fairness imaginable? In a word, have you not in every point been convinced out of your own mouth? And, if you can at present discover any flaw in any of your former concessions, or think of any remaining subterfuge, any new distinction, color, or comment whatsoever, why do you not produce it?

Hyl. A little patience, Philonous. I am at present so amazed to see myself ensnared, and as it were imprisoned in the labyrinths you have drawn me into, that on the sudden it cannot be expected I should find my way out. You must give me time to look about me and recollect myself.

Phil. Hark; is not this the college bell?

Hyl. It rings for prayers.

Phil. We will go in then, if you please, and meet here again to-morrow morning. In the meantime, you may employ your thoughts on this morning's discourse, and try if you can find any fallacy in it, or invent any new means to extricate yourself.

Hyl. Agreed.

THE SECOND DIALOGUE

Hyl. I beg your pardon, Philonous, for not meeting you sooner. All this morning my head was so filled with our late conversation, that I had not leisure to think of the time of the day, or indeed of anything else.

Phil. I am glad you were so intent upon it, in hopes if there were any mistakes in your concessions, or fallacies in my reasonings from them, you will now discover them to me.

Hyl. I assure you, I have done nothing ever since I saw you, but search after mistakes and fallacies, and with that view have minutely examined the whole series of yesterday's discourse: but all in vain, for the notions it led me into, upon review appear still more clear and evident; and the more I consider them, the more irresistibly do they force my assent.

Phil. And is not this, think you, a sign that they are genuine, that they proceed from nature, and are conformable to right reason? Truth and beauty are in this alike, that the strictest survey sets them both off to advantage. While the false luster of error and disguise cannot endure being reviewed, or too nearly inspected.

Hyl. I own there is a great deal in what you say. Nor can any one be more entirely satisfied of the truth of those odd consequences, so long as I have in view the reasonings that lead to them. But when these are out of my thoughts, there seems on the other hand, something so satisfactory, so natural and intelligible in the modern way of explaining things, that I profess I know not how to reject it.

Phil. I know not what way you mean.

Hyl. I mean the way of accounting for our sensations or ideas.

Phil. How is that?

Hyl. It is supposed the soul makes her residence in some part of the brain, from which the nerves take their rise, and are thence extended to all parts of the body: and that outward objects by the different impressions they make on the organs of sense, communicate certain vibrative motions to the nerves; and these being filled with spirits, propagate them to the brain or seat of the soul, which, according to the various impressions or traces thereby made in the brain, is variously affected with ideas.

Phil. And you call this an explication of the manner whereby we are affected with ideas?

Hyl.   Why not, Philonous, have you anything to object against it?

Phil.   I would first know whether I rightly understand your hypothesis. You make certain traces in the brain to be the causes or occasions of our ideas. Pray tell me, whether by the *brain* you mean any sensible thing.

Hyl.   What else think you I could mean?

Phil.   Sensible things are all immediately perceivable; and those things which are immediately perceivable, are ideas; and these exist only in the mind. Thus much you have, if I mistake not, long since agreed to.

Hyl.   I do not deny it.

Phil.   The brain therefore you speak of, being a sensible thing, exists only in the mind. Now, I would fain know whether you think it reasonable to suppose, that one idea or thing existing in the mind occasions all other ideas. And if you think so, pray how do you account for the origin of that primary idea or brain itself?

Hyl.   I do not explain the origin of our ideas by that brain which is perceivable to sense, this being itself only a combination of sensible ideas, but by another which I imagine.

Phil.   But are not things imagined as truly in the mind as things perceived?

Hyl.   I must confess they are.

Phil.   It comes therefore to the same thing; and you have been all this while accounting for ideas, by certain motions or impressions of the brain, that is, by some alterations in an idea, whether sensible or imaginable it matters not.

Hyl.   I begin to suspect my hypothesis.

Phil.   Besides spirits, all that we know or conceive are our own ideas. When therefore you say, all ideas are occasioned by impressions in the brain, do you conceive this brain or no? If you do, then you talk of ideas imprinted in an idea, causing that same idea, which is absurd. If you do not conceive it, you talk unintelligibly, instead of forming a reasonable hypothesis.

Hyl.   I now clearly see it was a mere dream. There is nothing in it.

Phil.   You need not be much concerned at it: for after all, this way of explaining things, as you called it, could never have satisfied any reasonable man. What connection is there between a motion in the nerves, and the sensations of sound or color in the mind? Or how is it possible these should be the effect of that?

Hyl.   But I could never think it had so little in it, as now it seems to have.

Phil.   Well then, are you at length satisfied that no sensible things have a real existence; and that you are in truth an arrant *skeptic*?

Hyl.   It is too plain to be denied.

Phil.   Look! Are not the fields covered with a delightful verdure? Is there not something in the woods and groves, in the rivers and clear springs that soothes, that delights, that transports the soul? At the prospect of the wide and deep ocean, or some huge mountain whose top is lost in the clouds, or of an old gloomy forest, are not our minds filled with a pleasing horror? Even in rocks and deserts, is there not an agreeable wildness? How sincere a pleasure is it to behold the natural beauties of the earth! To preserve and renew our relish for them, is not the veil of night alternately drawn over her face, and does she not change her dress with the seasons? How aptly are the elements disposed? What variety and use in the meanest productions of nature? What delicacy, what beauty, what contrivance in animal and vegetable bodies? How exquisitely are all things suited, as well to their particular ends, as to constitute opposite parts of the whole! And while they mutually aid and support, do they not also set off and illustrate each other? Raise now your thoughts from this ball of earth, to all those glorious luminaries that adorn the high arch of heaven. The motion and situation of the planets, are they not admirable for use and order? Were those (miscalled *erratic*) globes once known to stray, in their repeated journeys through the pathless void? Do they not measure areas round the sun ever proportioned to the times? So fixed, so immutable are the laws by which the unseen author of nature actuates the universe. How vivid and radiant is the luster of the fixed stars! How magnificent and rich that negligent profusion, with which they appear to be scattered throughout the whole azure vault! Yet if you take the telescope, it brings into your sight a new host of stars that escape the naked eye. Here they seem contiguous and minute, but to a nearer view immense orbs of light at various distances, far sunk in the abyss of space. Now you must call imagination to your aid. The feeble narrow sense cannot descry innumerable worlds revolving round the central fires; and in those worlds the energy of an all-perfect mind displayed in endless forms. But neither sense nor imagination are big enough to comprehend the boundless extent with all its glittering furniture. Though the laboring mind exert and strain each power to its upmost reach, there still stands out ungrasped a surplusage immeasurable. Yet all the vast bodies that compose this mighty frame, how distant and remote soever, are by some secret mechanism, some divine art and force, linked in a mutual dependence and intercourse with each other, even with this earth, which was almost slipped from my thoughts, and lost in the crowd of worlds. Is not the whole system immense, beautiful, glorious beyond expression and beyond thought! What treatment then do those philosophers deserve, who would deprive these noble and delightful scenes of all reality? How should those principles be entertained, that lead us to think all the visible beauty of the creation a false imaginary glare? To be plain, can you expect this skepticism of yours will not be thought extravagantly absurd by all men of sense?

Hyl. Other men may think as they please: but for your part you have nothing to reproach me with. My comfort is, you are as much a *skeptic* as I am.

Phil. There, Hylas, I must beg leave to differ from you.

Hyl. What! Have you all along agreed to the premises, and do you now deny the conclusion, and leave me to maintain those paradoxes by myself which you led me into? This surely is not fair.

Phil. I deny that I agreed with you in those notions that led to skepticism. You indeed said, the *reality* of sensible things consisted in an *absolute existence out of the minds of spirits,* or distinct from their being perceived. And pursuant to this notion of reality, *you* are obliged to deny sensible things any real existence: that is, according to your own definition, you profess yourself a *skeptic.* But I neither said nor thought the reality of sensible things was to be defined after that manner. To me it is evident, for the reasons you allow of, that sensible things cannot exist otherwise than in a mind or spirit. Whence I conclude, not that they have no real existence, but that seeing they depend not on my thought, and have an existence distinct from being perceived by me, *there must be some other mind wherein they exist.* As sure therefore as the sensible world really exists, so sure is there an infinite omnipresent spirit who contains and supports it.

Hyl. What! This is no more than I and all Christians hold; nay, and all others too who believe there is a God, and that he knows and comprehends all things.

Phil. Aye, but here lies the difference. Men commonly believe that all things are known or perceived by God, because they believe the being of a God; whereas I on the other side, immediately and necessarily conclude the being of a God, because all sensible things must be perceived by him.

  Hyl. But so long as we all believe the same thing, what matter is it how we come by that belief?

  Phil. But neither do we agree in the same opinion. For philosophers, though they acknowledge all corporeal beings to be perceived by God, yet they attribute to them an absolute subsistence distinct from their being perceived by any mind whatever, which I do not. Besides, is there no difference between saying, *There is a God, therefore he perceives all things:* and saying, *Sensible things do really exist: and, if they really exist, they are necessarily perceived by an infinite mind: therefore there is an infinite mind, or God.* This furnishes you with a direct and immediate demonstration, from a most evident principle, of the *being of a God.* Divines and philosophers had proved beyond all controversy, from the beauty and usefulness of the several parts of the creation, that it was the workmanship of God. But that setting aside all help of astronomy and natural philosophy, all contemplation of the contrivance, order, and adjustment of things, an infinite mind should be necessarily inferred from the bare existence of the sensible world, is an advantage to them only who have made this easy reflection: that the sensible world is that which we perceive by our several senses; and that nothing is perceived by the senses beside ideas; and that no idea or archetype of an idea can exist otherwise than in a mind. You may now, without any laborious search into the sciences, without any subtlety of reason, or tedious length of discourse, oppose and baffle the most strenuous advocate for atheism. Those miserable refuges, whether in an eternal succession of unthinking causes and effects, or in a fortuitous concourse of atoms; those wild imaginations of Vanini, Hobbes, and Spinoza: in a word the whole system of atheism, is it not entirely overthrown, by this single reflection on the repugnancy included in supposing the whole, or any part, even the most rude and shapeless of the visible world, to exist without a mind? Let any one of those abettors of impiety but look into his own thoughts, and then try if he can conceive how so much as a rock, a desert, a chaos, or confused jumble of atoms; how anything at all, either sensible or imaginable, can exist independent of a mind, and he need go no farther to be convinced of his folly. Can anything be fairer than to put a dispute on such an issue, and leave it to a man himself to see if he can conceive, even in thought, what he holds to be true in fact, and from a notional to allow it a real existence?

Hyl. It cannot be denied there is something highly serviceable to religion in what you advance. But do you not think it looks very like a notion entertained by some eminent moderns, of *seeing all things in God*?

Phil. I would gladly know that opinion; pray explain it to me.

Hyl. They conceive that the soul being immaterial, is incapable of being united with material things, so as to perceive them in themselves, but that she perceives them by her union with the substance of God, which being spiritual is therefore purely intelligible, or capable of being the immediate object of a spirit's thought. Besides, the divine essence contains in it perfections correspondent to each created being; and which are for that reason proper to exhibit or represent them to the mind.

Phil. I do not understand how our ideas, which are things altogether passive and inert, can be the essence, or any part (or like any part) of the essence or substance of God, who is an impassive, indivisible, purely active being. Many more difficulties and objections there are, which occur at first view against this hypothesis; but I shall only add that it is liable to all the absurdities of the common hypothesis, in making a created world exist otherwise than in the mind of a spirit. Beside all which it has this peculiar to itself; that it makes that material world serve to no purpose. And if it pass for a good argument against other hypotheses in the sciences, that they suppose nature, or the divine wisdom, to make something in vain, or do that by tedious roundabout methods, which might have been performed in a much more easy and compendious way, what shall we think of that hypothesis which supposes the whole world made in vain?

Hyl. But what say you, are not you too of opinion that we see all things in God? If I mistake not, what you advance comes near it.

Phil. [Few men think, yet all will have opinions. Hence men's opinions are superficial and confused. It is nothing strange that tenets, which in themselves are ever so different, should nevertheless be confounded with each other by those who do not consider them attentively. I shall not therefore be surprised if some men imagine that I run into the enthusiasm of Malebranche, though in truth I am very remote from it. He builds on the most abstract general ideas, which I entirely disclaim. He asserts an absolute external world, which I deny. He maintains that we are deceived by our senses, and know not the real natures or the true forms and figures of extended beings; of all which I hold the direct contrary. So that upon the whole there are no principles more fundamentally opposite than his and mine. It must be owned]* I entirely agree with what the holy Scripture says, *that in God we live and move and have our being*. But that we see things in his essence after the manner above set forth, I am far from believing. Take here in brief my meaning. It is evident that the things I perceive are my own ideas, and that no idea can exist unless it be in a mind. Nor is it less plain that these ideas or things by me perceived, either themselves or their archetypes, exist independently of my mind, since I know myself not to be their author, it being out of my power to determine at pleasure, what particular ideas I shall be affected with upon opening my eyes or ears. They must therefore exist in some other mind, whose will it is they should be exhibited to me. The things, I say, immediately perceived, are ideas or sensations, call them which you will. But how can any idea or sensation exist in, or be produced by, anything but a mind or spirit? This indeed is inconceivable; and to assert that which is inconceivable is to talk nonsense: is it not?

Hyl.   Without doubt.

Phil.   But on the other hand, it is very conceivable that they should exist in, and be produced by, a spirit; since this is no more than I daily experience in myself, inasmuch as I perceive numberless ideas; and by an act of my will can form a great variety of them, and raise them up in my imagination: though it must be confessed, these creatures of the fancy are not altogether so distinct, so strong, vivid, and permanent, as those perceived by my senses, which latter are called *real things*. From all which I conclude, *there is a mind which affects me every moment with all the sensible impressions I perceive*. And from the variety, order, and manner of these, I conclude the Author of them to be *wise, powerful, and good, beyond comprehension*. Mark it well; I do not say, I see things by perceiving that which represents them in the intelligible substance of God. This I do not understand; but I say, the things by me perceived are known by the understanding, and produced by the will, of an infinite spirit. And is not all this most plain and evident? Is there any more in it, than what a little observation in our own minds, and that which passes in them not only enables us to conceive, but also obliges us to acknowledge?

Hyl.   I think I understand you very clearly; and own the proof you give of a deity seems no less evident, than it is surprising. But allowing that God is the supreme and universal cause of all things, yet

---

* Added in the third edition.

may there not be still a third nature besides spirits and ideas? May we not admit a subordinate and limited cause of our ideas? In a word, may there not for all that be *matter*?

Phil. How often must I inculcate the same thing? You allow the things immediately perceived by sense to exist nowhere without the mind: but there is nothing perceived by sense, which is not perceived immediately: therefore there is nothing sensible that exists without the mind. The matter therefore which you still insist on, is something intelligible, I suppose; something that may be discovered by reason, and not by sense.

Hyl. You are in the right.

Phil. Pray let me know what reasoning your belief of matter is grounded on; and what this matter is in your present sense of it.

Hyl. I find myself affected with various ideas, whereof I know I am not the cause; neither are they the cause of themselves, or of one another, or capable of subsisting by themselves, as being altogether inactive, fleeting, dependent beings. They have therefore some cause distinct from me and them: of which I pretend to know no more, than that it is *the cause of my ideas*. And this thing, whatever it be, I call matter.

Phil. Tell me, Hylas, has every one a liberty to change the current proper signification attached to a common name in any language? For example, suppose a traveller should tell you, that in a certain country men might pass unhurt through the fire; and, upon explaining himself, you found he meant by the word *fire* that which others call *water*: or if he should assert that there are trees that walk upon two legs, meaning men by the term *trees*. Would you think this reasonable?

Hyl. No; I should think it very absurd. Common custom is the standard of propriety in language. And for any man to affect speaking improperly, is to pervert the use of speech, and can never serve to a better purpose, than to protract and multiply disputes where there is no difference in opinion.

Phil. And does not matter, in the common current acceptation of the word, signify an extended, solid, movable, unthinking, inactive substance?

Hyl. It does.

Phil. And has it not been made evident, that no such substance can possibly exist? And though it should be allowed to exist, yet how can that which is *inactive* be a *cause*; or that which is *unthinking* be a *cause of thought?* You may indeed, if you please, annex to the word *matter* a contrary meaning to what is vulgarly received; and tell me you understand by it, an unextended, thinking, active being, which is the cause of our ideas. But what else is this, than to play with words, and run into that very fault you just now condemned with so much reason? I do by no means find fault with your reasoning, in that you collect a cause from the phenomena: but I deny that the cause deducible by reason can properly be termed *matter*.

Hyl. There is indeed something in what you say. But I am afraid you do not thoroughly comprehend my meaning. I would by no means be thought to deny that God or an infinite spirit is the supreme cause of all things. All I contend for, is, that subordinate to the supreme agent there is a cause of a limited and inferior nature, which concurs in the production of our ideas, not by any act of will or spiritual efficiency, but by that kind of action which belongs to matter, *viz. motion.*

Phil. I find, you are at every turn relapsing into your old exploited conceit, of a moveable and consequently an extended substance existing without the mind. What! Have you already forgotten you were convinced, or are you willing I should repeat what has been said on that head? In truth this is not fair dealing in you, still to suppose the being of that which you have so often acknowledged to have no being. But not to insist farther on what has been so largely handled, I ask whether all your ideas are not perfectly passive and inert, including nothing of action in them.

Hyl. They are.

Phil. And are sensible qualities anything else but ideas?

Hyl. How often have I acknowledged that they are not.

Phil. But is not motion a sensible quality?

Hyl. It is.

Phil. Consequently it is no action?

Hyl. I agree with you. And indeed it is very plain, that when I stir my finger, it remains passive; but my will which produced the motion, is active.

Phil. Now I desire to know in the first place, whether motion being allowed to be no action, you can conceive any action besides volition: and in the second place, whether to say something and conceive nothing be not to talk nonsense: and lastly, whether having considered the premises, you do not perceive that to suppose any efficient or active cause of our ideas, other than *spirit*, is highly absurd and unreasonable?

Hyl. ~ I give up the point entirely. But though matter may not be a cause, yet what hinders its being an *instrument* subservient to the supreme agent in the production of our ideas?

Phil. An instrument, say you; pray what may be the figure, springs, wheels, and motions, of that instrument?

Hyl. Those I pretend to determine nothing of, both the substance and its qualities being entirely unknown to me.

Phil. What? Your are then of opinion, it is made up of unknown parts, that it has unknown motions, and an unknown shape?

Hyl. I do not believe that it has any figure or motion at all, being already convinced, that no sensible qualities can exist in an unperceiving substance.

Phil. But what notion is it possible to frame of an instrument void of all sensible qualities, even extension itself?

Hyl. I do not pretend to have any notion of it.

Phil. And what reason have you to think, this unknown, this inconceivable somewhat does exist? Is it that you imagine God cannot act as well without it, or that you find by experience the use of some such thing, when you form ideas in your own mind?

Hyl. You are always teasing me for reason of my belief. Pray, what reasons have you not to believe it?

Phil. It is to me a sufficient reason not to believe the existence of any thing, if I see no reason for believing it. But not to insist on reasons for believing, you will not so much as let me know what it is you would have me believe, since you say you have no manner of notion of it. After all, let me entreat you to consider whether it be like a philosopher, or even like a man of common sense, to pretend to believe you know not what, and you know not why.

Hyl. Hold, Philonous. When I tell you matter is an *instrument*, I do not mean altogether nothing. It is true, I know not the particular kind of instrument; but however I have some notion of *instrument in general*, which I apply to it.

Phil. But what if it should prove that there is something, even in the most general notion of *instrument*, as taken in a distinct sense from *cause*, which makes the use of it inconsistent with the divine attributes?

Hyl. Make that appear, and I shall give up the point.

Phil. What mean you by the general nature or notion of *instrument*?

Hyl. That which is common to all particular instruments, composes the general notion.

Phil. Is it not common to all instruments, that they are applied to the doing those things only, which cannot be performed by the mere act of our wills? Thus for instance, I never use an instrument to move my finger, because it is done by a volition. But I should use one, if I were to remove part of a rock, or tear up a tree by the roots. Are you of the same mind? Or can you show any example where an instrument is made use of in producing an effect immediately depending on the will of the agent?

Hyl. I own, I cannot.

Phil. How therefore can you suppose, that an all-perfect spirit, on whose will all things have an absolute and immediate dependence, should need an instrument in his operations, or not needing it make use of it? Thus it seems to me that you are obliged to own the use of a lifeless inactive instrument, to be incompatible with the infinite perfection of God; that is, by your own confession, to give up the point.

Hyl. It does not readily occur what I can answer you.

Phil. But methinks you should be ready to own the truth, when it has been fairly proved to you. We indeed, who are beings of finite powers, are forced to make use of instruments. And the use of an instrument shows the agent to be limited by rules of another's prescription, and that he cannot obtain his end, but in such a way and by such conditions. Whence it seems a clear consequence, that the supreme unlimited agent uses no tool or instrument at all. The will of an omnipotent spirit is no sooner exerted than executed, without the application of means, which, if they are employed by inferior agents, it is not upon account of any real efficacy that is in them, or necessary aptitude to produce any effect, but merely in compliance with the laws of nature, or those conditions prescribed to them by the first cause, who is himself above all limitation or prescription whatsoever.

Hyl. I will no longer maintain that matter is an instrument. However, I would not be understood to give up its existence neither; since, notwithstanding what has been said, it may still be an *occasion*.

Phil. How many shapes is your matter to take? Or how often must it be proved not to exist, before you are content to part with it? But to say no more of this (though by all the laws of disputation I may justly blame you for so frequently changing the signification of the principal term) I would fain know what you mean by affirming that matter is an occasion, having already denied it to be a cause. And when you have shown in what sense you understand *occasion*, pray in the next place be pleased to show me what reason induces you to believe there is such an occasion of our ideas.

Hyl. As to the first point: by *occasion* I mean an inactive unthinking being, at the presence whereof God excites ideas in our minds.

Phil. And what may be the nature of that inactive unthinking being?

Hyl. I know nothing of its nature.

Phil. Proceed then to the second point, and assign some reason why we should allow an existence to this inactive, unthinking, unknown thing.

Hyl. When we see ideas produced in our minds after an orderly and constant manner, it is natural to think they have some fixed and regular occasions, at the presence of which they are excited.

Phil. You acknowledge then God alone to be the cause of our ideas, and that he causes them at the presence of those occasions.

Hyl. That is my opinion.

Phil. Those things which you say are present to God, without doubt he perceives.

Hyl. Certainly; otherwise they could not be to him an occasion of acting.

Phil. Not to insist now on your making sense of this hypothesis, or answering all the puzzling questions and difficulties it is liable to: I only ask whether the order and regularity observable in the series of our ideas, or the course of nature, be not sufficiently accounted for by the wisdom and power of God; and whether it does not derogate from those attributes, to suppose he is influenced, directed, or put in mind, when and what he is to act, by any unthinking substance. And lastly whether, in case I granted all you contend for, it would make any thing to your purpose, it not being easy to conceive how the external or absolute existence of an unthinking substance, distinct from its being perceived, can be inferred from my allowing that there are certain things perceived by the mind of God, which are to him the occasion of producing ideas in us.

Hyl. I am perfectly at a loss what to think, this notion of *occasion* seeming now altogether as groundless as the rest.

Phil.   Do you not at length perceive, that in all these different acceptations of *matter*, you have been only supposing you know not what, for no manner of reason, and to no kind of use?

Hyl.   I freely own my self less fond of my notions, since they have been so accurately examined. But still, methinks I have some confused perception that there is such a thing as *matter*.

Phil.   Either you perceive the being of matter immediately, or mediately. If immediately, pray inform me by which of the senses you perceive it. If mediately, let me know by what reasoning it is inferred from those things which you perceive immediately. So much for the perception. Then for the matter itself, I ask whether it is object, *substratum*, cause, instrument, or occasion? You have already pleaded for each of these, shifting your notions, and making matter to appear sometimes in one shape, then in another. And what you have offered has been disapproved and rejected by yourself. If you have anything new to advance, I would gladly hear it.

Hyl.   I think I have already offered all I had to say on those heads. I am at a loss what more to urge.

Phil.   And yet you are loth to part with your old prejudice. But to make you quit it more easily, I desire that, beside what has been hitherto suggested, you will farther consider whether, upon supposition that matter exists, you can possibly conceive how you should be affected by it? Or supposing it did not exist, whether it be not evident you might for all that be affected with the same ideas you now are, and consequently have the very same reasons to believe its existence that you now can have?

Hyl.   I acknowledge it is possible we might perceive all things just as we do now, though there was no matter in the world; neither can I conceive, if there be matter, how it should produce any idea in our minds. And I do farther grant, you have entirely satisfied me, that it is impossible there should be such a thing as matter in any of the foregoing acceptations. But still I cannot help supposing that there is *matter* in some sense or other. What that is I do not indeed pretend to determine.

Phil.   I do not expect you should define exactly the nature of that unknown being. Only be pleased to tell me, whether it is a substance: and if so, whether you can suppose a substance without accidents; or in case you suppose it to have accidents or qualities, I desire you will let me know what those qualities are, at least what is meant by matter's supporting them.

Hyl.   We have already argued on those points. I have no more to say to them. But to prevent any farther questions, let me tell you, I at present understand by *matter* neither substance nor accident, thinking nor extended being, neither cause, instrument, nor occasion, but something entirely unknown, distinct from all these.

Phil.   It seems then you include in your present notion of matter, nothing but the general abstract idea of *entity*.

Hyl.   Nothing else, save only that I super-add to this general idea the negation of all those particular things, qualities, or ideas that I perceive, imagine, or in any wise apprehend.

Phil.   Pray where do you suppose this unknown matter to exist?

Hyl.   Oh Philonous! Now you think you have entangled me; for if I say it exists in place, then you will infer that it exists in the mind, since it is agreed, that place or extension exists only in the mind: but I am not ashamed to own my ignorance. I know not where it exists; only I am sure it exists not in place. There is a negative answer for you: and you must expect no other to all the questions you put for the future about matter.

Phil.   Since you will not tell me where it exists, be pleased to inform me after what manner you suppose it to exist, or what you mean by its *existence*.

Hyl.   It neither thinks nor acts, neither perceives, nor is perceived.

Phil.   But what is there positive in your abstracted notion of its existence?

Hyl.   Upon a nice observation, I do not find I have any positive notion or meaning at all. I tell you again I am not ashamed to own my ignorance. I know not what is meant by its *existence*, or how it exists.

Phil.   Continue, good Hylas, to act the same ingenuous part, and tell me sincerely whether you can frame a distinct idea of entity in general, prescinded from and exclusive of all thinking and corporeal beings, all particular things whatsoever.

Hyl.   Hold, let me think a little — I profess, Philonous, I do not find that I can. At first glance methought I had some dilute and airy notion of pure entity in abstract; but upon closer attention it has quite vanished out of sight. The more I think on it, the more am I confirmed in my prudent resolution of giving none but negative answers, and not pretending to the least degree of any positive knowledge or conception of matter, its *where*, its *how*, its *entity*, or any thing belonging to it.

Phil.   When therefore you speak of the existence of matter, you have not any notion in your mind.

Hyl.   None at all.

Phil.   Pray tell me if the case stands not thus: at first from a belief of material substance you would have it that the immediate objects existed without the mind; then that their archetypes; then cause; next instruments; then occasions; lastly, *something in general*, which being interpreted proves *nothing*. So matter comes to nothing. What think you, Hylas, is not this a fair summary of your whole proceeding?

Hyl.   Be that as it will, yet I still insist upon it, that our not being able to conceive a thing, is no argument against its existence.

Phil.   That from a cause, effect, operation, sign, or other circumstance, there may reasonably be inferred the existence of a thing not immediately perceived, and that it were absurd for any man to argue against the existence of that thing, from his having no direct and positive notion of it, I freely own. But where there is nothing of all this; where neither reason nor revelation induce us to believe the existence of a thing; where we have not even a relative notion of it; where an abstraction is made from perceiving and being perceived, from spirit and idea: lastly, where there is not so much as the most inadequate or faint idea pretended to: I will not indeed thence conclude against the reality of any notion or existence of any thing: but my inference shall be, that you mean nothing at all: that you employ words to no manner of purpose, without any design or signification whatsoever. And I leave it to you to consider how mere jargon should be treated.

Hyl.   To deal frankly with you, Philonous, your arguments seem in themselves unanswerable, but they have not so great an effect on me as to produce that entire conviction, that hearty acquiescence which attends demonstration. I find myself still relapsing into an obscure surmise of I know not what, *matter.*

Phil.   But are you not sensible, Hylas, that two things must concur to take away all scruple, and work a plenary assent in the mind? Let a visible object be set in never so clear a light, yet if there is any imperfection in the sight, or if the eye is not directed towards it, it will not be distinctly seen. And though a demonstration be never so well grounded and fairly proposed, yet if there is withal a stain of prejudice, or a wrong bias on the understanding, can it be expected on a sudden to perceive clearly and adhere firmly to the truth? No, there is need of time and pains: the attention must be awakened and detained by a frequent repetition of the same thing placed oft in the same, oft in different lights. I have said it already, and find I must still repeat and inculcate, that it is an unaccountable licence you take in pretending to maintain you know not what, for you know not what reason, to you know not what purpose? Can this be paralleled in any art or science, any sect or profession of men? Or is there any thing so barefacedly groundless and unreasonable to be met with even in the lowest of common conversation? But perhaps you will still say, matter may exist, though at the same time you neither know what is meant by *matter*, or by its *existence*. This indeed is surprising, and the more so because it is altogether voluntary, you not being led to it by any one reason; for I challenge you to show me that thing in nature which needs matter to explain or account for it.

Hyl. The reality of things cannot be maintained without supposing the existence of matter. And is not this, think you, a good reason why I should be earnest in its defence?

Phil. The reality of things! What things, sensible or intelligible?

Hyl. Sensible things.

Phil. My glove, for example?

Hyl. That or any other thing perceived by the senses.

Phil. But to fix on some particular thing; is it not a sufficient evidence to me of the existence of this *glove*, that I see it, and feel it, and wear it? Or if this will not do, how is it possible I should be assured of the reality of this thing, which I actually see in this place, by supposing that some unknown thing which I never did or can see, exists after an unknown manner, in an unknown place, or in no place at all? How can the supposed reality of that which is intangible, be a proof that any thing tangible really exists? Or of that which is invisible, that any visible thing, or in general of any thing which is imperceptible, that a perceptible exists? Do but explain this, and I shall think nothing too hard for you.

Hyl. Upon the whole, I am content to own the existence of matter is highly improbable; but the direct and absolute impossibility of it does not appear to me.

Phil. But granting matter to be possible, yet upon that account merely it can have no more claim to existence, than a golden mountain or a centaur.

Hyl. I acknowledge it; but still you do not deny it is possible; and that which is possible, for aught you know, may actually exist.

Phil.   I deny it to be possible; and have, if I mistake not, evidently proved from your own concessions that it is not. In the common sense of the word *matter*, is there any more implied, than an extended, solid, figured, moveable substance existing without the mind? And have not you acknowledged over and over, that you have seen evident reason for denying the possibility of such a substance?

Hyl.   True, but that is only one sense of the term *matter*.

Phil.   But is it not the only proper genuine received sense? And if matter in such a sense be proved impossible, may it not be thought with good grounds absolutely impossible? Else how could any thing be proved impossible? Or indeed how could there be any proof at all one way or other, to a man who takes the liberty to unsettle and change the common signification of words?

Hyl.   I thought philosophers might be allowed to speak more accurately than the vulgar, and were not always confined to the common acceptation of a term.

Phil.   But this now mentioned is the common received sense among philosophers themselves. But not to insist on that, have you not been allowed to take matter in what sense you pleased? And have you not used this privilege in the utmost extent, sometimes entirely changing, at others leaving out or putting into the definition of it whatever for the present best served your design, contrary to all the known rules of reason and logic? And has not this shifting unfair method of yours spun out our dispute to an unnecessary length; matter having been particularly examined, and by your own confession refuted in each of those senses? And can any more be required to prove the absolute impossibility of a thing, than the proving it impossible in every particular sense, that either you or any one else understands it in?

Hyl.   But I am not so thoroughly satisfied that you have proved the impossibility of matter in the last most obscure abstracted and indefinite sense.

Phil.   When is a thing shown to be impossible?

Hyl.   When a repugnancy is demonstrated between the ideas comprehended in its definition.

Phil.   But where there are no ideas, there no repugnancy can be demonstrated between ideas.

Hyl.   I agree with you.

Phil. Now in that which you call the obscure indefinite sense of the word *matter*, it is plain, by your own confession, there was included no idea at all, no sense except an unknown sense, which is the same thing as none. You are not therefore to expect I should prove a repugnancy between ideas where there are no ideas; or the impossibility of matter taken in an *unknown* sense, that is no sense at all. My business was only to show, you meant *nothing*; and this you were brought to own. So that in all your various senses, you have been showed either to mean nothing at all, or if any thing, an absurdity. And if this be not sufficient to prove the impossibility of a thing, I desire you will let me know what is.

Hyl. I acknowledge you have proved that matter is impossible; nor do I see what more can be said in defence of it. But at the same time that I give up this, I suspect all my other notions. For surely none could be more seemingly evident than this once was: and yet it now seems as false and absurd as ever it did true before. But I think we have discussed the point sufficiently for the present. The remaining part of the day I would willingly spend, in running over in my thoughts the several heads of this morning's conversation, and tomorrow shall be glad to meet you here again about the same time.

Phil. I will not fail to attend you.

THE THIRD DIALOGUE

Phil. Tell me, Hylas, what are the fruits of yesterday's meditation? Has it confirmed you in the same mind you were in at parting? Or have you since seen cause to change your opinion?

Hyl. Truly my opinion is, that all our opinions are alike vain and uncertain. What we approve today, we condemn tomorrow. We keep a stir about knowledge, and spend our lives in the pursuit of it, when, alas! we know nothing all the while: nor do I think it possible for us ever to know anything in this life. Our faculties are too narrow and too few. Nature certainly never intended us for speculation.

Phil. What! Say you we can know nothing, Hylas?

Hyl. There is not that single thing in the world, whereof we can know the real nature, or what it is in itself.

Phil. Will you tell me I do not really know what fire or water is?

Hyl. You may indeed know that fire appears hot, and water fluid: but this is no more than knowing what sensations are produced in your own mind, upon the application of fire and water to your organs of sense. Their internal constitution, their true and real nature, you are utterly in the dark as to *that*.

Phil. Do I not know this to be a real stone that I stand on, and that which I see before my eyes to be a real tree?

Hyl. *Know?* No, it is impossible you or any man alive should know it. All you know, is, that you have such a certain idea or appearance in your own mind. But what is this to the real tree or stone? I tell you, that color, figure, and hardness, which you perceive, are not the real natures of those things, or in the least like them. The same may be said of all other real things or corporeal substances which compose the world. They have none of them anything in themselves, like those sensible qualities by us perceived. We should not therefore pretend to affirm or know anything of them, as they are in their own nature.

Phil. But surely, Hylas, I can distinguish gold, for example, from iron: and how could this be, if I knew not what either truly was?

Hyl. Believe me, Philonous, you can only distinguish between your own ideas. That yellowness, that weight, and other sensible qualities, think you they are really in the gold? They are only relative to the senses, and have no absolute existence in nature. And in pretending to distinguish the species of real things, by the appearances in your mind, you may perhaps act as wisely as he that should conclude two men were of a different species, because their clothes were not of the same color.

Phil. It seems then we are altogether put off with the appearances of things, and those false ones too. The very meat I eat, and the cloth I wear, have nothing in them like what I see and feel.

Hyl. Even so.

Phil. But is it not strange the whole world should be thus imposed on, and so foolish as to believe their senses? And yet I know not how it is, but men eat, and drink, and sleep, and perform all the offices of life, as comfortably and conveniently, as if they really knew the things they are conversant about.

Hyl. They do so: but you know ordinary practice does not require a nicety of speculative knowledge. Hence the vulgar retain their mistakes, and for all that, make a shift to bustle through the affairs of life. But philosophers know better things.

Phil. You mean, they know that they *know nothing*.

Hyl. That is the very top and perfection of human knowledge.

Phil. But are you all this while in earnest, Hylas; and are you seriously persuaded that you know nothing real in the world? Suppose you are going to write, would you not call for pen, ink, and paper, like another man; and do you not know what it is you call for?

Hyl. How often must I tell you, that I know not the real nature of any one thing in the universe? I may indeed upon occasion make use of pen, ink, and paper. But what any one of them is in its own true nature, I declare positively I know not. And the same is true with regard to every other corporeal thing. And, what is more, we are not only ignorant of the true and real nature of things, but even of their existence. It cannot be denied that we perceive such certain appearances or ideas; but it cannot be concluded from thence that bodies really exist. Nay, now I think on it, I must agreeably to my former concessions farther declare, that it is impossible any real corporeal thing should exist in nature.

Phil. You amaze me. Was ever anything more wild and extravagant than the notions you now maintain: and is it not evident you are led into all these extravagancies by the belief of *material substance*? This makes you dream of those unknown natures in everything. It is this occasions your distinguishing between the reality and sensible appearances of things. It is to this you are indebted for being ignorant of what everybody else knows perfectly well. Nor is this all: you are not only ignorant of the true nature of everything, but you know not whether anything really exists, or whether there are any true natures at all; forasmuch as you attribute to your material beings an absolute or external existence, wherein you suppose their reality consists. And as you are forced in the end to acknowledge such an existence means either a direct repugnancy, or nothing at all, it follows that you are obliged to pull down your own hypothesis of material substance, and positively to deny the real existence of any part of the universe. And so you are plunged into the deepest and most deplorable *skepticism* that ever man was. Tell me, Hylas, is it not as I say?

    Hyl.   I agree with you. *Material substance* was no more than an hypothesis, and a false and groundless one too. I will no longer spend my breath in defence of it. But whatever hypothesis you advance, or whatsoever scheme of things you introduce in its stead, I doubt not it will appear every whit as false: let me but be allowed to question you upon it. That is, suffer me to serve you in your own kind, and I warrant it shall conduct you through as many perplexities and contradictions, to the very same state of skepticism that I myself am in at present.

    Phil.   I assure you, Hylas, I do not pretend to frame any hypothesis at all. I am of a vulgar cast, simple enough to believe my senses, and leave things as I find them. To be plain, it is my opinion, that the real things are those very things I see and feel, and perceive by my sense. These I know, and finding they answer all the necessities and purposes of life, have no reason to be solicitous about any other unknown beings. A piece of sensible bread, for instance, would stay my stomach better than ten thousand times as much of that insensible, unintelligible, real bread you speak of. It is likewise my opinion, that colors and other sensible qualities are on the objects. I cannot for my life help thinking that snow is white, and fire hot. You indeed, who by *snow* and *fire* mean certain external, unperceived, unperceiving substances, are in the right to deny whiteness or heat to be affections inherent in them. But I, who understand by those words the things I see and feel, am obliged to think like other folks. And as I am no skeptic with regard to the nature of things, so neither am I as to their existence. That a thing should be really perceived by my senses, and at the same time not really exist, is to me a plain contradiction; since I cannot prescind or abstract, even in thought, the existence of a sensible thing from its being perceived. Wood, stones, fire, water, flesh, iron, and the like things, which I name and discourse of, are things that I know. And

I should not have known them, but that I perceived them by my senses; and things perceived by the senses are immediately perceived; and things immediately perceived are ideas; and ideas cannot exist without the mind; their existence therefore consists in being perceived; when therefore they are actually perceived, there can be no doubt of their existence. Away then with all that skepticism, all those ridiculous philosophical doubts. What a jest is it for a philosopher to question the existence of sensible things, till he has it proved to him from the veracity of God: or to pretend our knowledge in this point falls short of intuition or demonstration? I might as well doubt of my own being, as of the being of those things I actually see and feel.

Hyl.   Not so fast, Philonous: you say you cannot conceive how sensible things should exist without the mind. Do you not?

Phil.   I do.

Hyl.   Supposing you were annihilated, cannot you conceive it possible, that things perceivable by sense may still exist?

Phil.   I can; but then it must be in another mind. When I deny sensible things an existence out of the mind, I do not mean my mind in particular, but all minds. Now it is plain they have an existence exterior to my mind, since I find them by experience to be independent of it. There is therefore some other mind wherein they exist, during the intervals between the times of my perceiving them: as likewise they did before my birth, and would do after my supposed annihilation. And as the same is true, with regard to all other finite created spirits; it necessarily follows, there is an *omnipresent eternal mind*, which knows and comprehends all things, and exhibits them to our view in such a manner, and according to such rules as he himself has ordained, and are by us termed the *laws of nature*.

Hyl.   Answer me, Philonous. Are all our ideas perfectly inert beings? Or have they any agency included in them?

Phil.   They are altogether passive and inert.

Hyl.   And is not God an agent, a being purely active?

Phil.   I acknowledge it.

Hyl.   No idea therefore can be like unto, or represent the nature of God.

Phil.   It cannot.

Hyl.   Since therefore you have no idea of the mind of God, how can you conceive it possible, that things should exist in his mind? Or, if you can conceive the mind of God without having an idea of it, why may not I be allowed to conceive the existence of matter, notwithstanding that I have no idea of it?

Phil. As to your first question; I own I have properly no idea, either of God or any other spirit; for these being active, cannot be represented by things perfectly inert, as our ideas are. I do nevertheless know, that I, who am a spirit or thinking substance, exist as certainly, as I know my ideas exist. Farther, I know what I mean by the terms *I* and *myself*; and I know this immediately, or intuitively, though I do not perceive it as I perceive a triangle, a color, or a sound. The mind, spirit, or soul, is that indivisible unextended thing, which thinks, act, and perceives. I say *indivisible*, because unextended; and *unextended*, because extended, figured, moveable things, are ideas; and that which perceives ideas, which thinks and wills, is plainly itself no idea, nor like an idea. Ideas are things inactive, and perceived: and spirits a sort of beings altogether different from them. I do not therefore say my soul is an idea, or like an idea. However, taking the word *idea* in a large sense, my soul may be said to furnish me with an idea, that is, an image, or likeness of God, though indeed extremely inadequate. For all the notion I have of God, is obtained by reflecting on my own soul, heightening its powers, and removing its imperfections. I have therefore, though not an inactive idea, yet in myself some sort of an active thinking image of the Deity. And though I perceive him not by sense, yet I have a notion of him, or know him by reflection and reasoning. My own mind and my own ideas I have an immediate knowledge of; and by the help of these, do mediately apprehend the possibility of the existence of other spirits and ideas. Farther, from my own being, and from the dependency I find in myself and my ideas, I do by an act of reason, necessarily infer the existence of a God, and of all created things in the mind of God. So much for your first question. For the second: I suppose by this time you can answer it yourself. For you neither perceive matter objectively, as you do an inactive being or idea, nor know it, as you do yourself, by a reflex act: neither do you mediately apprehend it by similitude of the one or the other: nor yet collect it by reasoning from that which you know immediately. All which makes the case of *matter* widely different from that of the *Deity*.

[*Hyl.* You say your own soul supplies you with some sort of an idea or image of God. But at the same time you acknowledge you have, properly speaking, no idea of your own soul. You even affirm that spirits are a sort of beings altogether different from ideas. Consequently that no idea can be like a spirit. We have therefore no idea of any spirit. You admit nevertheless that there is spiritual substance, although you have no idea of it; while you deny there can be such a thing as material substance, because you have no notion or idea of it. Is this fair dealing? To act consistently, you must either admit matter or reject spirit. What say you to this?

Phil.   I say in the first place, that I do not deny the existence of material substance, merely because I have no notion of it, but because the notion of it is inconsistent, or in other words, because it is repugnant that there should be a notion of it. Many things, for aught I know, may exist, whereof neither I nor any other man has or can have any idea or notion whatsoever. But then those things must be possible, that is, nothing inconsistent must be included in their definition. I say secondly, that although we believe things to exist which we do not perceive; yet we may not believe that any particular thing exists, without some reason for such belief: but I have no reason for believing the existence of matter. I have no immediate intuition thereof: neither can I mediately from my sensations, ideas, notions, actions or passions, infer an unthinking, unperceiving, inactive substance, either by probable deduction, or necessary consequence. Whereas the being of my self, that is, my own soul, mind or thinking principle, I evidently know by reflection. You will forgive me if I repeat the same things in answer to the same objections. In the very notion or definition of material substance, there is included a manifest repugnance and inconsistency. But this cannot be said of the notion of spirit. That ideas should exist in what does not perceive, or be produced by what does not act, is repugnant. But it is no repugnancy to say, that a perceiving thing should be the subject of ideas, or an active thing the cause of them. It is granted we have neither an immediate evidence nor a demonstrative knowledge of the existence of other finite spirits; but it will not thence follow that such spirits are on a foot with material substances: if to suppose the one be inconsistent, and it be not inconsistent to suppose the other; if the one can be inferred by no argument, and there is a probability for the other; if we see signs and effects indicating distinct finite agents like ourselves, and see no sign or symptom whatever that leads to a rational belief of matter. I say lastly, that I have a notion of spirit, though I have not, strictly speaking, an idea of it. I do not perceive it as an idea or by means of an idea, but know it by reflection.

66

Hyl. Notwithstanding all you have said, to me it seems, that according to your own way of thinking, and in consequence of your own principles, it should follow that you are only a system of floating ideas, without any substance to support them. Words are not to be used without a meaning. And as there is no more meaning in spiritual substance than in material substance, the one is to be exploded as well as the other.

Phil. How often must I repeat, that I know or am conscious of my own being; and that I myself am not my ideas, but somewhat else, a thinking active principle that perceives, knows, wills, and operates about ideas. I know that I, one and the same self, perceive both colors and sounds: that a color cannot perceive a sound, nor a sound a color: that I am therefore one individual principle, distinct from color and sound; and, for the same reason, from all other sensible things and inert ideas. But I am not in like manner conscious either of the existence or essence of matter. On the contrary, I know that nothing inconsistent can exist, and that the existence of matter implies an inconsistency. Farther, I know what I mean, when I affirm that there is a spiritual substance or support of ideas, that is, that a spirit knows and perceives ideas. But I do not know what is meant, when it is said, that an unperceiving substance has inherent in it and supports either ideas or the archetypes of ideas. There is therefore upon the whole no parity of case between spirit and matter.] *

Hyl. I own myself satisfied in this point. But do you in earnest think, the real existence of sensible things consists in their being actually perceived? If so; how comes it that all mankind distinguish between them? Ask the first man you meet, and he shall tell you, *to be perceived* is one thing, and *to exist* is another.

Phil. I am content, Hylas, to appeal to the common sense of the world for the truth of my notion. Ask the gardener, why he thinks yonder cherry tree exists in the garden, and he shall tell you, because he sees and feels it; in a word, because he perceives it by his senses. Ask him why he thinks an orange tree not to be there, and he shall tell you, because he does not perceive it. What he perceives by sense, that he terms a real being, and says it *is*, or *exists*; but that which is not perceivable, the same, he says, has no being.

Hyl. Yes, Philonous, I grant the existence of a sensible thing consists in being perceivable, but not in being actually perceived.

---

* Added in third edition.

Phil.   And what is perceivable but an idea? And can an idea exist without being actually perceived? These are points long since agreed between us.

Hyl.   But be your opinion never so true, yet surely you will not deny it is shocking, and contrary to the common sense of men. Ask the fellow, whether yonder tree has an existence out of his mind: what answer think you he would make?

Phil.   The same that I should myself, to wit, that it does exist out of his mind. But then to a Christian it cannot surely be shocking to say, the real tree existing without his mind is truly known and comprehended by (that is, *exists in*) the infinite mind of God. Probably he may not at first glance be aware of the direct and immediate proof there is of this, inasmuch as the very being of a tree, or any other sensible thing, implies a mind wherein it is. But the point itself he cannot deny. The question between the materialists and me is not, whether things have a real existence out of the mind of this or that person, but whether they have an absolute existence, distinct from being perceived by God, and exterior to all minds. This indeed some heathens and philosophers have affirmed, but whoever entertains notions of the Deity suitable to the Holy Scriptures, will be of another opinion.

Hyl.   But according to your notions, what difference is there between real things, and chimeras formed by the imagination, or the visions of a dream, since they are all equally in the mind?

Phil.   The ideas formed by the imagination are faint and indistinct; they have, besides, an entire dependence on the will. But the ideas perceived by sense, that is, real things, are more vivid and clear, and being imprinted on the mind by a spirit distinct from us, have not a like dependence on our will. There is therefore no danger of confounding these with the foregoing: and there is as little of confounding them with the visions of a dream, which are dim, irregular, and confused. And though they should happen to be never so lively and natural, yet by their not being connected, and of a piece with the preceding and subsequent transactions of our lives, they might easily be distinguished from realities. In short, by whatever method you distinguish *things* from *chimeras* on your own scheme, the same, it is evident, will hold also upon mine. For it must be, I presume, by some perceived difference, and I am not for depriving you of any one thing that you perceive.

Hyl. But still, Philonous, you hold, there is nothing in the world but spirits and ideas. And this, you must needs acknowledge, sounds very oddly.

Phil. I own the word *idea*, not being commonly used for *thing*, sounds something out of the way. My reason for using it was, because a necessary relation to the mind is understood to be implied by that term; and it is now commonly used by philosophers, to denote the immediate objects of the understanding. But however oddly the proposition may sound in words, yet it includes nothing so very strange or shocking in its sense, which in effect amounts to no more than this, to wit, that there are only things perceiving, and things perceived; or that every unthinking being is necessarily, and from the very nature of its existence, perceived by some mind; if not by any finite created mind, yet certainly by the infinite mind of God, in whom *we live, and move, and have our being.* * Is this as strange as to say, the sensible qualities are not on the objects: or, that we cannot be sure of the existence of things, or know anything of their real natures, though we both see and feel them, and perceive them by all our senses?

Hyl. And in consequence of this, must we not think there are no such things as physical or corporeal causes; but that a spirit is the immediate cause of all the *phenomena* in nature? Can there be anything more extravagant than this?

Phil. Yes, it is infinitely more extravagant to say, a thing which is inert, operates on the mind, and which is unperceiving, is the cause of our perceptions. Besides, that which to you, I know not for what reason, seems so extravagant, is no more than the Holy Scriptures assert in a hundred places. In them God is represented as the sole and immediate author of all those effects, which some heathens and philosophers are wont to ascribe to nature, matter, fate, or the like unthinking principle. This is so much the constant language of Scripture, that it were needless to confirm it by citations.

Hyl. You are not aware, Philonous, that in making God the immediate author of all the motions in nature, you make him the author of murder, sacrilege, adultery, and the like heinous sins.

Phil. In answer to that, I observe first, that the imputation of guilt is the same, whether a person commits an action with or without an

---

* *Acts* 17:28.

instrument. In case therefore you suppose God to act by the mediation of an instrument, or occasion, called *matter*, you as truly make him the author of sin as I, who think him the immediate agent in all those operations vulgarly ascribed to nature. I farther observe, that sin or moral turpitude does not consist in the outward physical action or motion, but in the internal deviation of the will from the laws of reason and religion. This is plain, in that the killing an enemy in a battle, or putting a criminal legally to death, is not thought sinful, though the outward act be the very same with that in the case of murder. Since therefore sin does not consist in the physical action, the making God an immediate cause of all such actions, is not making him the author of sin. Lastly, I have nowhere said that God is the only agent who produces all the motions in bodies. It is true, I have denied there are any other agents beside spirits: but this is very consistent with allowing to thinking rational beings, in the production of motions, the use of limited powers, ultimately indeed derived from God, but immediately under the direction of their own wills, which is sufficient to entitle them to all the guilt of their actions.

Hyl. But the denying matter, Philonous, or corporeal substance; there is the point. You can never persuade me that this is not repugnant to the universal sense of mankind. Were our dispute to be determined by most voices, I am confident you would give up the point, without gathering the votes.

Phil. I wish both our opinions were fairly stated and submitted to the judgment of men who had plain common sense, without the prejudices of a learned education. Let me be represented as one who trusts his senses, who thinks he knows the things he sees and feels, and entertains no doubts of their existence; and you fairly set forth with all your doubts, your paradoxes, and your skepticism about you, and I shall willingly acquiesce in the determination of any indifferent person. That there is no substance wherein ideas can exist beside spirit, is to me evident. And that the objects immediately perceived are ideas, is on all hands agreed. And that sensible qualities are objects immediately perceived, no one can deny. It is therefore evident there can be no *substratum* of those qualities but spirit, in which they exist, not by way of mode or property, but as thing perceived in that which perceives it. I deny therefore that there is any unthinking *substratum* of the objects of sense, and in that acceptation that there is any material substance. But if by *material substance* is meant only sensible body, that which is seen and felt (and the unphilosophical part of the world, I dare say, mean no more) then I am more certain of matter's existence than you, or any other philosopher, pretend to be. If there be anything which makes the generality of mankind averse from the notions I espouse, it is a misapprehension that I deny the reality of sensible things: but as it is you who are guilty of that and not I, it follows that in truth their aversion is against your notions, and not mine. I do therefore assert that I am as certain as of my own being, that there are bodies or corporeal substances, (meaning the things I perceive by my senses) and that granting this, the bulk of mankind will take no thought about, nor think themselves at all concerned in the fate of those unknown natures, and philosophical quiddities, which some men are so fond of.

Hyl. What say you to this? Since, according to you, men judge of the reality of things by their senses, how can a man be mistaken in thinking the moon a plain lucid surface, about a foot in diameter; or a square tower, seen at a distance, round; or an oar, with one end in the water, crooked?

Phil. He is not mistaken with regard to the ideas he actually perceives; but in the inferences he makes from his present perceptions. Thus in the case of the oar, what he immediately perceives by sight is certainly crooked; and so far he is in the right. But if he thence conclude, that upon taking the oar out of the water he shall perceive the same crookedness; or that it would affect his touch, as crooked things are wont to do: in that he is mistaken. In like manner, if he shall conclude from what he perceives in one station, that in case he advances toward the moon or tower, he should still be affected with the like ideas, he is mistaken. But his mistake lies not in what he perceives immediately and at present (it being a manifest contradiction to suppose he should err in respect of that) but in the wrong judgment he makes concerning the ideas he apprehends to be connected with those immediately perceived: or concerning the ideas that, from what he perceives at present, he imagines would be perceived in other circumstances. The case is the same with regard to the Copernican system. We do not here perceive any motion of the earth: but it were erroneous thence to conclude, that in case we were placed at as great a distance from that, as we are now from the other planets, we should not then perceive its motion.

Hyl. I understand you; and must needs own you say things plausible enough: but give me leave to put you in mind of one thing. Pray, Philonous, were you not formerly as positive that matter existed, as you are now that it does not?

Phil. I was. But here lies the difference. Before, my positiveness was founded without examination, upon prejudice; but now, after inquiry, upon evidence.

Hyl. After all, it seems our dispute is rather about words than things. We agree in the thing, but differ in the name. That we are affected with ideas from without is evident; and it is no less evident, that there must be (I will not say archetypes, but) powers without the mind, corresponding to those ideas. And as these powers cannot subsist by themselves, there is some subject of them necessarily to be admitted which I call *matter,* and you call *spirit.* This is all the difference.

Phil. Pray, Hylas, is that powerful being, or subject of powers, extended?

Hyl. It has not extension; but has the power to raise in you the idea of extension.

Phil. It is therefore itself unextended.

Hyl. I grant it.

Phil. Is it not also active?

Hyl. Without doubt: otherwise, how could we attribute powers to it?

Phil. Now let me ask you two questions: *first,* whether it be agreeable to the usage either of philosophers or others, to give the name *matter* to an unextended active being? And *secondly,* whether it be not ridiculously absurd to misapply names contrary to the common use of language?

Hyl. Well then, let it not be called matter, since you will have it so, but some *third nature* distinct from matter and spirit. For, what reason is there why you should call it spirit? Does not the notion of spirit imply, that it is thinking as well as active and unextended?

Phil. My reason is this: because I have a mind to have some notion of meaning in what I say; but I have no notion of any action distinct from volition, neither can I conceive volition to be anywhere but in a spirit: therefore when I speak of an active being, I am obliged to mean a spirit. Beside, what can be plainer than that a thing which has no ideas in itself, cannot impart them to me; and if it has ideas, surely it must be a spirit. To make you comprehend the point still more clearly if it be possible: I assert as well as you, that since we are affected from without, we must allow powers to be without in a being distinct from ourselves. So far we are agreed. But then we differ as to the kind of this powerful being. I will have it to be spirit, you matter, or I know not what (I may add too, you know not what) third nature. Thus I prove it to be spirit. From the effects I see produced, I conclude there are actions; and because actions, volitions; and because there are volitions, there must be a will. Again, the things I perceive must have an existence, they or their archetypes, out of my mind: but being ideas, neither they nor their archetypes can exist otherwise than in an understanding: there is therefore an understanding. But will and understanding constitute in the strictest sense a mind or spirit. The powerful cause therefore of my ideas, is in strict propriety of speech a *spirit*.

    Hyl.   And now I warrant you think you have made the point very clear, little suspecting that what you advance leads directly to a contradiction. Is it not an absurdity to imagine any imperfection in God?

    Phil.   Without a doubt.

    Hyl.   To suffer pain is an imperfection.

    Phil.   It is.

    Hyl.   Are we not sometimes affected with pain and uneasiness by some other being?

    Phil.   We are.

    Hyl.   And have you not said that being is a spirit, and is not that spirit God?

    Phil.   I grant it.

    Hyl.   But you have asserted, that whatever ideas we perceive from without, are in the mind which affects us. The ideas therefore of pain and uneasiness are in God; or in other words, God suffers pain: that is to say, there is an imperfection in the divine nature, which you acknowledged was absurd. So you are caught in a plain contradiction.

    Phil.   That God knows or understands all things, and that he knows among other things what pain is, even every sort of painful sensation, and what it is for his creatures to suffer pain, I make no question. But that God, though he knows and sometimes causes painful sensations in us, can himself suffer pain, I positively deny. We who are limited and dependent spirits, are liable to impressions of sense, the effects of an external agent, which being produced against our wills, are sometimes painful and uneasy. But God, whom no external being can affect, who perceives nothing by sense as we do, whose will is absolute and independent, causing all things, and liable to be thwarted or resisted by nothing; it is evident, such a being as this can suffer nothing, nor be affected with any painful sensation, or indeed any sensation at all. We are chained to a body, that is to say, our perceptions are connected with corporeal motions. By the law of our nature we are affected upon every alteration in the nervous parts of our sensible body: which sensible body, rightly considered, is nothing but a complection of such qualities or ideas, as have no existence distinct from being perceived by a mind: so that this connection of sensations with corporeal motions, means no more than a correspondence in the order of nature between two sets of ideas, or things immediately perceivable. But God is a pure spirit, disengaged from all such sympathy or natural ties. No corporeal motions are attended with the sensation of pain or pleasure in his mind. To know everything knowable is certainly a perfection; but to endure, or suffer, or feel anything by sense, is an imperfection. The former, I say, agrees to God, but not the latter. God knows, or has ideas; but his ideas are not conveyed to him by sense, as ours are. Your not distinguishing, where there is so manifest a difference, makes you fancy you see an absurdity where there is none.

Hyl.   But all this while you have not considered, that the quantity of matter has been demonstrated to be proportioned to the gravity of bodies. And what can withstand demonstration?

Phil.   Let me see how you demonstrate that point.

Hyl.   I lay it down for a principle, that the moments or quantities of motion in bodies, are in a direct compounded reason of the velocities and quantities of matter contained in them. Hence, where the velocities are equal, it follows, the moments are directly as the quantity of matter in each. But it is found by experience, that all bodies (bating the small inequalities, arising from the resistance of the air) descend with an equal velocity; the motion therefore of descending bodies, and consequently their gravity, which is the cause or principle of that motion, is proportional to the quantity of matter; which was to be demonstrated.

Phil.   You lay it down as a self-evident principle, that the quantity of motion in any body, is proportional to the velocity and *matter* taken together: and this is made use of to prove a proposition, from whence the existence of *matter* is inferred. Pray is not this arguing in a circle?

Hyl.   In the premise I only mean, that the motion is proportional to the velocity, jointly with the extension and solidity.

Phil.   But allowing this to be true, yet it will not thence follow, that gravity is proportional to *matter*, in your philosophic sense of the word;

except you take it for granted, that unknown *substratum*, or whatever else you call it, is proportional to those sensible qualities; which to suppose, is plainly begging the question. That there is magnitude and solidity, or resistance, perceived by sense, I readily grant; as likewise that gravity may be proportional to those qualities, I will not dispute. But that either these qualities as perceived by us, or the powers producing them, do exist in a *material substratum;* this is what I deny, and you indeed affirm, but notwithstanding your demonstration, have not yet proved.

Hyl. I shall insist no longer on that point. Do you think, however, you shall persuade me the natural philosophers have been dreaming all this while; pray what becomes of all their hypotheses and explications of the *phenomena,* which suppose the existence of matter?

Phil. What mean you, Hylas, by the *phenomena?*

Hyl. I mean the appearances which I perceive by my senses.

Phil. And the appearances perceived by sense, are they not ideas?

Hyl. I have told you so a hundred times.

Phil. Therefore, to explain the *phenomena,* is to show how we come to be affected with ideas, in that manner and order wherein they are imprinted on our senses. Is it not?

Hyl. It is.

Phil. Now if you can prove, that any philosopher has explained the production of any one idea in our minds by the help of *matter,* I shall for ever acquiesce and look on all that has been said against it as nothing: but if you cannot, it is vain to urge the explication of *phenomena.* That a being endowed with knowledge and will, should produce or exhibit ideas, is easily understood. But that a being which is utterly destitute of these faculties should be able to produce ideas, or in any sort to affect an intelligence, this I can never understand. This I say, though we had some positive conception of matter, though we knew its qualities, and could comprehend its existence, would yet be so far from explaining things, that it is itself the most inexplicable thing in the world. And yet for all this, it will not follow, that philosophers have been doing nothing; for by observing and reasoning upon the connection of ideas, they discover the laws and methods of nature, which is a part of knowledge both useful and entertaining.

Hyl. After all, can it be supposed God would deceive all mankind? Do you imagine, he would have induced the whole world to believe the being of matter, if there was no such thing?

Phil. That every epidemical opinion arising from prejudice, or passion, or thoughtlessness, may be imputed to God, as the author of it, I believe you will not affirm. Whatsoever opinion we father on him, it must be either because he has discovered it to us by supernatural revelation, or because it is so evident to our natural faculties, which were framed and given us by God, that it is impossible we should withhold our assent from it. But where is the revelation? Or where is the evidence that extorts the belief of matter? Nay, how does it appear, that matter taken for something distinct from what we perceive by our senses, is thought to exist by all mankind, or indeed by any except a few philosophers, who do not know what they would be at? Your question supposes these points are clear; and when you have cleared them, I shall think myself obliged to give you another answer. In the meantime let it suffice that I tell you, I do not suppose God has deceived mankind at all.

Hyl. But the novelty, Philonous, the novelty! There lies the danger. New notions should always be discountenanced; they unsettle men's minds, and nobody knows where they will end.

Phil. Why the rejecting a notion that has no foundation either in sense or in reason, or in divine authority, should be thought to unsettle the belief of such opinions as are grounded on all or any of these, I cannot imagine. That innovations in government and religion, are dangerous, and ought to be discountenanced, I freely own. But is there the like reason why they should be discouraged in philosophy? The making anything known which was unknown before, is an innovation in knowledge: and if all such innovations had been forbidden, men would* have made a notable progress in the arts and sciences. But it is none of my business to plead for novelties and paradoxes. That the qualities we perceive, are not on the objects: that we must not believe our senses: that we know nothing of the real nature of things, and can never be assured even of their existence: that real colors and sounds are nothing but certain unknown figures and motions: that motions are in themselves neither swift nor slow: that there are in bodies absolute extensions, without any particular magnitude or figure: that a thing stupid, thoughtless and inactive, operates

---

* A *not* may have been omitted here in all three original editions.

on a spirit: that the least particle of a body, contains innumerable extended parts. These are the novelties, these are the strange notions which shock the genuine uncorrupted judgment of all mankind; and being once admitted, embarrass the mind with endless doubts and difficulties. And it is against these and the like innovations, I endeavor to vindicate common sense. It is true, in doing this, I may perhaps be obliged to use some *ambages*, and ways of speech not common. But if my notions are once thoroughly understood, that which is most singular in them, will in effect be found to amount to no more than this: that it is absolutely impossible, and a plain contradiction to suppose, any unthinking being should exist without being perceived by a mind. And if this notion be singular, it is a shame it should be so at this time of day, and in a Christian country.

Hyl. As for the difficulties other opinions may be liable to, those are out of the question. It is your business to defend your own opinion. Can anything be plainer, than that you are for changing all things into ideas? You, I say, who are not ashamed to charge me with *skepticism*. This is so plain, there is no denying it.

Phil. You mistake me. I am not for changing things into ideas, but rather ideas into things; since those immediate objects of perception, which according to you, are only appearances of things, I take to be the real things themselves.

Hyl. Things! You may pretend what you please; but it is certain, you leave us nothing but the empty forms of things, the outside only which strikes the senses.

Phil. What you call the empty forms and outside of things, seems to me the very things themselves. Nor are they empty or incomplete otherwise, than upon your supposition, that matter is an essential part of all corporeal things. We both therefore agree in this, that we perceive only sensible forms: but herein we differ, you will have them to be empty appearances, I real beings. In short you do not trust your senses, I do.

Hyl. You say you believe your senses; and seem to applaud yourself that in this you agree with the vulgar. According to you therefore, the true nature of a thing is discovered by the senses. If so, whence comes that disagreement? Why is not the same figure, and other sensible qualities, perceived all manner of ways? And why should we use a microscope, the better to discover the true nature of a body, if it were discoverable to the naked eye?

Phil.   Strictly speaking, Hylas, we do not see the same object that we feel; neither is the same object perceived by the microscope, which was by the naked eye. But in case every variation was thought sufficient to constitute a new kind or individual, the endless number or confusion of names would render language impracticable. Therefore to avoid this as well as other inconveniencies which are obvious upon a little thought, men combine together several ideas, apprehended by divers senses, or by the same sense at different times, or in different circumstances, but observed however to have some connection in nature, either with respect to co-existence or succession; all which they refer to one name, and consider as one thing. Hence it follows that when I examine by my other senses a thing I have seen, it is not in order to understand better the same object which I had perceived by sight, the object of one sense not being perceived by the other senses. And when I look through a microscope, it is not that I may perceive more clearly what I perceived already with my bare eyes, the object perceived by the glass being quite different from the former. But in both cases my aim is only to know what ideas are connected together; and the more a man knows of the connection of ideas, the more he is said to know of the nature of things. What therefore if our ideas are variable; what if our senses are not in all circumstances affected with the same appearances? It will not thence follow, they are not to be trusted, or that they are inconsistent either with themselves or anything else, except it be with your preconceived notion of (I know not what) one single, unchanged, unperceivable, real nature, marked by each name: which prejudice seems to have taken its rise from not rightly understanding the common language of men speaking of several distinct ideas, as united into one thing by the mind. And indeed there is cause to suspect several erroneous conceits of the philosophers are owing to the same original: while they began to build their schemes, not so much on notions as words, which were framed by the vulgar, merely for conveniency and dispatch in the common actions of life, without any regard to speculation.

Hyl.   Methinks I apprehend your meaning.

Phil.   It is your opinion, the ideas we perceive by our senses are not real things, but images, or copies of them. Our knowledge therefore is no farther real, than as our ideas are the true representations of those originals. But as these supposed originals are in themselves unknown, it is impossible to know how far our ideas resemble them; or whether they resemble them at all. We cannot therefore be sure we have any real knowledge. Farther, as our ideas are perpetually varied, without any change in the supposed real things, it necessarily follows they cannot all be true copies of them: or if some are, and others are not, it is impossible to distinguish the former from the latter. And this plunges us yet deeper in uncertainty. Again, when we consider the point, we cannot conceive how any idea, or anything like an idea, should have an absolute existence out of a mind: nor consequently, according to you, how there should be any real thing in nature. The result of all which is, that we are thrown into the most hopeless and abandoned *skepticism*. Now give me leave to ask you, *first*, whether your referring ideas to certain absolutely existing unperceived substances, as their originals, be not the source of all this *skepticism? Secondly*, whether you are informed, either by sense or reason, of the existence of those unknown originals? And in case you are not, whether it be not absurd to suppose them? *Thirdly*, whether, upon inquiry, you find there is anything distinctly conceived or meant by the *absolute or external existence of unperceiving substances? Lastly*, whether the premises considered, it be not the wisest way to follow nature, trust your senses, and laying aside all anxious thought about unknown natures or substances, admit with the vulgar those for real things, which are perceived by the senses?

    Hyl.   For the present, I have no inclination to the answering part. I would much rather see how you can get over what follows. Pray are not the objects perceived by the senses of one, likewise perceivable to others present? If there were an hundred more here, they would all see the garden, the trees, and flowers as I see them. But they are not in the same manner affected with the ideas I frame in my imagination. Does not this make a difference between the former sort of objects and the latter?

    Phil.   I grant it does. Nor have I ever denied a difference between the objects of sense and those of imagination. But what would you infer from thence? You cannot say that sensible objects exist unperceived, because they are perceived by many.

    Hyl.   I own I can make nothing of that objection: but it has led me into another. Is it not your opinion that by our senses we perceive only the ideas existing in our minds?

    Phil.   It is.

    Hyl.   But the same idea which is in my mind, cannot be in yours, or in any other mind. Does it not therefore follow from your principles, that no two can see the same thing? And is not this highly absurd?

Phil.   If the term *same* be taken in the vulgar acceptation, it is certain (and not at all repugnant to the principles I maintain) that different persons may perceive the same thing; or the same thing or idea exist in different minds. Words are of arbitrary imposition; and since men are used to apply the word *same* where no distinction or variety is perceived, and I do not pretend to alter their perceptions, it follows, that as men have said before, *several saw the same thing,* so they may upon like occasions still continue to use the same phrase, without any deviation either from propriety of language, or the truth of things. But if the term *same* be used in the acceptation of philosophers, who pretend to an abstracted notion of identity, then, according to their sundry definitions of this notion (for it is not yet agreed wherein that philosophic identity consists) it may or may not be possible for divers persons to perceive the same thing. But whether philosophers shall think fit to call a thing the *same* or no, is, I conceive, of small importance. Let us suppose several men together, all endued with the same faculties, and consequently affected in like sort by their senses, and who had yet never known the use of language; they would without question agree in their perceptions. Though perhaps, when they came to the use of speech, some regarding the uniformness of what was perceived, might call it the *same* thing: others especially regarding the diversity of persons who perceived, might choose the denomination of different things. But who sees not that all the dispute is about a word? To wit, whether what is perceived by different persons, may yet have the term *same* applied to it? Or suppose a house, whose walls or outward shell remaining unaltered, the chambers are all pulled down and new ones built in their place; and that you should call this the *same,* and I should say it was not the *same* house: would we not for all this perfectly agree in our thoughts of the house, considered in itself? And would not all the difference consist in a sound? If you should say, we differed in our notions; for that you superadded to your idea of the house the simple abstracted idea of identity, whereas I did not; I would tell you I know not what you mean by that *abstracted idea of identity;* and should desire you to look into your own thoughts, and be sure you understood yourself. — Why so silent, Hylas? Are you not yet satisfied, men may dispute about identity and diversity, without any real difference in their thoughts and opinions, abstracted from names? Take this farther reflection with you: that whether matter be allowed to exist or no, the case is exactly the same as to the point in hand. For the materialists themselves acknowledge what we immediately perceive by our senses, to be our own ideas. Your difficulty therefore, that no two see the same thing, makes equally against the materialists and me.

Hyl. But they suppose an external archetype, to which referring their several ideas, they may truly be said to perceive the same thing.

Phil. And (not to mention your having discarded those archetypes) so may you suppose an external archetype on my principles; *external,* I mean, to your own mind; though indeed it must be supposed to exist in that mind which comprehends all things; but then this serves all the ends of identity, as well as if it existed out of a mind. And I am sure you yourself will not say, it is less intelligible.

Hyl. You have indeed clearly satisfied me, either that there is no difficulty at bottom in this point; or if there be, that it makes equally against both opinions.

Phil. But that which makes equally against two contradictory opinions, can be a proof against neither.

Hyl. I acknowledge it. But after all, Philonous, when I consider the substance of what you advance against *skepticism,* it amounts to no more than this. We are sure that we really see, hear, feel; in a word, that we are affected with sensible impressions.

Phil. And how are we concerned any farther? I see this *cherry,* I feel it, I taste it: and I am sure *nothing* cannot be seen, or felt, or tasted: it is therefore *real.* Take away the sensations of softness, moisture, redness, tartness, and you take away the *cherry.* Since it is not a being distinct from sensations; a *cherry,* I say, is nothing but a congeries of sensible impressions, or ideas perceived by various senses: which ideas are united into one thing (or have one name given them) by the mind; because they are observed to attend each other. Thus when the palate is affected with such a particular taste, the sight is affected with a red color, the touch with roundness, softness, &c. Hence, when I see, and feel, and taste, in such sundry certain manners, I am sure the *cherry* exists, or is real; its reality being in my opinion nothing abstracted from those sensations. But if by the word *cherry* you mean an unknown nature distinct from all those sensible qualities, and by its existence something distinct from its being perceived; then indeed I own, neither you nor I, nor any one else, can be sure it exists.

Hyl. But what would you say, Philonous, if I should bring the very same reasons against the existence of sensible things in a mind, which you have offered against their existing in a material *substratum?*

Phil. When I see your reasons, you shall hear what I have to say to them.

Hyl. Is the mind extended or unextended?

Phil. Unextended, without doubt.

Hyl. Do you say the things you perceive are in your mind?

Phil. They are.

Hyl. Again, have I not heard you speak of sensible impressions?

Phil. I believe you may.

Hyl. Explain to me now, O Philonous! how it is possible there should be room for all those trees and houses to exist in your mind. Can extended things be contained in that which is unextended? Or are we to imagine impressions made on a thing void of all solidity? You cannot say objects are in your mind, as books in your study: or that things are imprinted on it, as the figure of a seal upon wax. In what sense therefore are we to understand those expressions? Explain me this if you can: and I shall then be able to answer all those queries you formerly put to me about my *substratum.*

Phil. Look you, Hylas, when I speak of objects as existing in the mind or imprinted on the senses; I would not be understood in the gross literal sense, as when bodies are said to exist in a place, or a seal to make an impression upon wax. My meaning is only that the mind comprehends or perceives them; and that it is affected from without, or by some being distinct from itself. This is my explication of your difficulty; and how it can serve to make your tenet of an unperceiving material *substratum* intelligible, I would fain know.

Hyl. Nay, if that be all, I confess I do not see what use can be made of it. But are you not guilty of some abuse of language in this?

Phil. None at all: it is no more than common custom, which you know is the rule of language, has authorized: nothing being more usual, than for philosophers to speak of the immediate objects of the understanding as things existing in the mind. Nor is there anything in this, but what is conformable to the general analogy of language; most part of the mental operations being signified by words borrowed from sensible things; as is plain in the terms *comprehend, reflect, discourse, &c.,* which, being applied to the mind, must not be taken in their gross, original sense.

Hyl. You have, I own, satisfied me in this point: but there still remains one great difficulty, which I know not how you will get over. And indeed it is of such importance, that if you could solve all others, without being able to find a solution for this, you must never expect to make me a proselyte to your principles.

Phil. Let me know this mighty difficulty.

Hyl. The Scripture account of the creation, is what appears to me utterly irreconcilable with your notions. Moses tells us of a creation: a creation of what? Of ideas? No certainly, but of things, of real things, solid corporeal substances. Bring your principles to agree with this, and I shall perhaps agree with you.

Phil. Moses mentions the sun, moon, and stars, earth and sea, plants and animals: that all these do really exist, and were in the beginning created by God, I make no question. If by *ideas,* you mean fictions and fancies of the mind, then these are no ideas. If by *ideas* you mean immediate objects of the understanding, or sensible things which cannot exist unperceived, or out of a mind, then these things are ideas. But whether you do, or do not call them *ideas,* it matters little. The difference is only about a name. And whether that name be retained or rejected, the sense, the truth and reality of things continues the same. In common talk, the objects of our senses are not termed *ideas* but *things.* Call them so still: provided you do not attribute to them any absolute external existence, and I shall never quarrel with you for a word. The creation therefore I allow to have been a creation of things, of *real* things. Neither is this in the least inconsistent with my principles, as is evident from what I have now said; and would have been evident to you without this, if you had not forgotten what had been so often said before. But as for solid corporeal substances, I desire you to show where Moses makes any mention of them; and if they should be mentioned by him, or any other inspired writer, it would still be incumbent on you to show those words were not taken in the vulgar acceptation for things falling under our senses, but in the philosophic acceptation, for matter, or an unknown quiddity, with an absolute existence. When you have proved these points, then (and not till then) may you bring the authority of Moses into our dispute.

Hyl. It is in vain to dispute about a point so clear. I am content to refer it to your own conscience. Are you not satisfied there is some peculiar repugnancy between the Mosaic account of the creation, and your notions?

Phil.   If all possible sense, which can be put on the first chapter of *Genesis*, may be conceived as consistently with my principles as any other, then it has no peculiar repugnancy with them. But there is no sense you may not as well conceive, believing as I do. Since, beside spirits, all you conceive are ideas; and the existence of these I do not deny. Neither do you pretend they exist without the mind.

Hyl.   Pray let me see any sense you can understand it in.

Phil.   Why, I imagine that if I had been present at the creation, I should have seen things produced into beings; that is, become perceptible, in the order described by the sacred historian. I ever before believed the Mosaic account of the creation, and now find no alteration in my manner of believing it. When things are said to begin or end their existence, we do not mean this with regard to God, but his creatures. All objects are eternally known by God, or which is the same thing, have an eternal existence in his mind: but when things, before imperceptible to creatures, are by a decree of God, made perceptible to them; then are they said to begin a relative existence, with respect to created minds. Upon reading therefore the Mosaic account of the creation, I understand that the several parts of the world became gradually perceivable to finite spirits, endowed with proper faculties; so that whoever such were present, they were in truth perceived by them. This is the literal obvious sense suggested to me, by the words of the Holy Scripture: in which is included no mention or no thought, either of *substratum*, instrument, occasion, or absolute existence. And upon inquiry, I doubt not, it will be found, that most plain honest men, who believe the creation, never think of those things any more than I. What metaphysical sense you may understand it in, you only can tell.

Hyl.   But, Philonous, you do not seem to be aware, that you allow created things in the beginning, only a relative, and consequently, hypothetical being: that is to say, upon supposition there were men to perceive them, without which they have no actuality of absolute existence, wherein creation might terminate. Is it not therefore according to you plainly impossible, the creation of any inanimate creatures should precede that of man? And is not this directly contrary to the Mosaic account?

Phil.   In answer to that I say, *first*, created beings might begin to exist in the mind of other created intelligences, beside men. You will not therefore be able to prove any contradiction between Moses and my notions, unless you first show, there was no other order of finite created spirits in being before man. I say farther, in case we conceive the creation, as we should at this time a parcel of plants or vegetables of all sorts, produced by an invisible power, in a desert where nobody was present: that this way of explaining or conceiving it, is consistent with my principles, since they deprive you of nothing, either sensible or imaginable: that it exactly suits with the common, natural, undebauched notions of mankind: that it manifests the dependence of all things on God; and consequently has all the good effect or influence, which it is possible that important article of our faith should have in making men humble, thankful, and resigned to their creator. I say moreover, that in this naked conception of things, divested of words, there will not be found any notion of what you call the *actuality of absolute existence*. You may indeed raise a dust with those terms, and so lengthen our dispute to no purpose. But I entreat you calmly to look into your own thoughts, and then tell me if they are not an useless and unintelligible jargon.

Hyl. I own, I have no very clear notion annexed to them. But what say you to this? Do you not make the existence of sensible things consist in their being in a mind? And were not all things eternally in the mind of God? Did they not therefore exist from all eternity, according to you? And how could that which was eternal, be created in time? Can anything be clearer or better connected than this?

Phil. And are not you too of opinion, that God knew all things from eternity?

Hyl. I am.

Phil. Consequently they always had a being in the divine intellect.

Hyl. This I acknowledge.

Phil. By your own confession therefore, nothing is new, or begins to be, in respect of the mind of God. So we are agreed in that point.

Hyl. What shall we make then of the creation?

Phil. May we not understand it to have been entirely in respect of finite spirits; so that things, with regard to us, may properly be said to begin their existence, or be created, when God decreed they should become perceptible to intelligent creatures, in that order and manner which he then established, and we now call the laws of nature? You may call this a *relative,* or *hypothetical existence* if you please. But so long as it supplies us with the most natural, obvious, and literal sense of the Mosaic history of the creation; so long as it answers all the religious ends of that great article; in a word, so long as you can assign no other sense or meaning in its stead; why should we reject this? Is it to comply with a ridiculous skeptical humor of making everything nonsense and unintelligible? I am sure you cannot say, it is for the glory of God. For allowing it to be a thing possible and conceivable, that the corporeal world should have an absolute subsistence extrinsical to the mind of God, as well as to the minds of all created spirits: yet how could this set forth either the immensity or omniscience of the Deity, or the necessary and immediate dependence of all things on him? Nay, would it not rather seem to derogate from those attributes?

Hyl. Well, but as to this decree of God's, for making things perceptible: what say you, Philonous, is it not plain, God did either execute that decree from all eternity, or at some certain time began to will what he had not actually willed before, but only designed to will. If the former, then there could be no creation or beginning of existence in finite things. If the latter, then we must acknowledge something new to befall the Deity; which implies a sort of change: and all change argues imperfection.

Phil. Pray consider what you are doing. Is it not evident, this objection concludes equally against a creation in any sense; nay, against every other act of the Deity, discoverable by the light of nature? None of which can we conceive, otherwise than as performed in time, and having a beginning. God is a being of transcendent and unlimited perfections: his nature therefore is incomprehensible to finite spirits. It is not therefore to be expected, that any man, whether *materialist* or *immaterialist,* should have exactly just notions of the Deity, his attributes, and ways of operation. If then you would infer anything against me, your difficulty must not be drawn from the inadequateness of our conceptions of the divine nature, which is unavoidable on any scheme; but from the denial of matter, of which there is not one word, directly or indirectly, in what you have now objected.

Hyl. I must acknowledge, the difficulties you are concerned to clear, are such only as arise from the non-existence of matter, and are peculiar to that notion. So far you are in the right. But I cannot by any means bring myself to think there is no such peculiar repugnancy between the creation and your opinion; though indeed where to fix it, I do not distinctly know.

Phil. What would you have! Do I not acknowledge a twofold state of things, the one ectypal or natural, the other archetypal and eternal? The former was created in time; the latter existed from everlasting in the mind of God. Is not this agreeable to the common notions of divines? Or is any more than this necessary in order to conceive the creation? But you suspect some peculiar repugnancy, though you know not where it lies. To take away all possibility of scruple in the case, do but consider this one point. Either you are not able to conceive the creation on any hypothesis whatsoever; and if so, there is no ground for dislike or complaint against my particular opinion on that score: or you are able to conceive it; and, if so, why not on my principles, since thereby nothing conceivable is taken away? You have all along been allowed the full scope of sense, imagination, and reason. Whatever therefore you could before apprehend, either immediately or mediately by your sense, or by ratiocination from your sense; whatever you could perceive, imagine, or understand, remains still with you. If therefore the notion you have of the creation by other principles be intelligible, you have it still upon mine; if it be not intelligible, I conceive it to be no notion at all; and so there is no loss of it. And indeed it seems to me very plain, that the supposition of matter, that is, a thing perfectly unknown and inconceivable, cannot serve to make us conceive anything. And I hope, it need not be proved to you, that if the existence of matter does not make the creation conceivable, the creation's being without it inconceivable, can be no objection against its non-existence.

Hyl.   I confess, Philonous, you have almost satisfied me in this point of the creation.

Phil.   I would fain know why you are not quite satisfied. You tell me indeed of a repugnancy between the Mosaic history and immaterialism: but you know not where it lies. Is this reasonable, Hylas? Can you expect I should solve a difficulty without knowing what it is? But to pass by all that, would not a man think you were assured there is no repugnancy between the received notions of materialists and the inspired writings?

Hyl.   And so I am.

Phil.   Ought the historical part of Scripture to be understood in a plain obvious sense, or in a sense which is metaphysical, and out of the way?

Hyl.   In the plain sense, doubtless.

Phil.   When Moses speaks of herbs, earth, water, &c. as having been created by God; think you not the sensible things, commonly signified by those words, are suggested to every unphilosophical reader?

Hyl.　I cannot help thinking so.

Phil.　And are not all ideas, or things perceived by sense, to be denied a real existence by the doctrine of the materialists?

Hyl.　True.

Phil.　Is it not therefore evident, the asserters of matter destroy the plain obvious sense of Moses, with which their notions are utterly inconsistent; and instead of it obtrude on us I know not what, something equally unintelligible to themselves and me?

Hyl.　I cannot contradict you.

Phil.　Moses tells us of a creation. A creation of what? Of unknown quiddities, of occasions, or *substratums?* No certainly; but of things obvious to the senses. You must first reconcile this with your notions, if you expect I should be reconciled to them.

Hyl.　I see you can assault me with my own weapons.

Phil.　Then as to *absolute existence;* was there ever known a more jejune notion than that? Something it is, so abstracted and unintelligible, that you have frankly owned you could not conceive it, much less explain anything by it. But allowing matter to exist, and the notion of absolute existence to be as clear as light; yet was this ever known to make the creation more credible? Nay has it not furnished the *atheists* and *infidels* of all ages, with the most plausible argument against a creation? That a corporeal substance, which has an absolute existence without the minds of spirits, should be produced out of nothing by the mere will of a spirit, has been looked upon as a thing so contrary to all reason, so impossible and absurd, that not only the most celebrated among the ancients, but even divers modern and Christian philosophers have thought matter co-eternal with the Deity. Lay these things together, and then judge you whether materialism disposes men to believe the creation of things.

Hyl.　I own, Philonous, I think it does not. This of the *creation* is the last objection I can think of; and I must needs own it has been sufficiently answered as well as the rest. Nothing now remains to be overcome, but a sort of unaccountable backwardness that I find in myself toward your notions.

Phil.　When a man is swayed, he knows not why, to one side of the question; can this, think you, be anything else but the effect of prejudice, which never fails to attend old and rooted notions? And indeed in this respect I cannot deny the belief of matter to have very much the advantage over the contrary opinion, with men of a learned education.

Hyl.   I confess it seems to be as you say.

Phil.   As a balance therefore to this weight of prejudice, let us throw into the scale the great advantages that arise from the belief of immaterialism, both in regard to religion and human learning. The being of a God, and incorruptibility of the soul, those great articles of religion, are they not proved with the clearest and most immediate evidence? When I say the being of a *God*, I do not mean an obscure general cause of things, whereof we have no conception, but *God*, in the strict and proper sense of the word. A being whose spirituality, omnipresence, providence, omniscience, infinite power and goodness, are as conspicuous as the existence of sensible things, of which (notwithstanding the fallacious pretences and affected scruples of *skeptics*) there is no more reason to doubt, than of our own being. Then with relation to human sciences; in natural philosophy, what intricacies, what obscurities, what contradictions, has the belief of matter led men into! To say nothing of the numberless disputes about its extent, continuity, homogeneity, gravity, divisibility, &c. do they not pretend to explain all things by bodies operating on bodies, according to the laws of motion? And yet, are they able to comprehend how any one body should move another? Nay, admitting there was no difficulty in reconciling the notion of an inert being with a cause; or in conceiving how an accident might pass from one body to another; yet by all their strained thoughts and extravagant supposition, have they been able to reach the mechanical production of any one animal or vegetable body? Can they account, by the laws of motion, for sounds, tastes, smells, or colors, or for the regular course of things? Have they accounted by physical principles for the aptitude and contrivance, even of the most inconsiderable parts of the universe? But laying aside matter and corporeal causes, and admitting only the efficiency of an all-perfect mind, are not all the effects of nature easy and intelligible? If the *phenomena* are nothing else but *ideas;* God is a *spirit*, but matter an unintelligent, unperceiving being. If they demonstrate an unlimited power in their cause; God is active and omnipotent, but matter an inert mass. If the order, regularity, and usefulness of them, can never be sufficiently admired; God is infinitely wise and provident, but matter destitute of all contrivance and design. These surely are great advantages in *physics*. Not to mention that the apprehension of a distant deity, naturally disposes men to a negligence in their *moral* actions, which they would be more cautious of, in case they thought him immediately present, and acting on their minds without the interposition of matter, or unthinking second causes. Then in *metaphysics;* what difficulties concerning entity in abstract, substantial forms, hylarchic principles, plastic natures, substance and accident, principle of individuation, possibility of matter's thinking, origin of ideas, the manner how two independent substances, so widely different as *spirit* and *matter,* should mutually operate on each other? What difficulties, I say, and endless disquisitions concerning these and innumerable other the like points, do we escape by supposing only spirits and ideas? Even the *mathematics* themselves, if we take away the absolute existence of extended things, become much more clear and easy; the most shocking paradoxes and intricate speculations in those sciences, depending on the infinite divisibility of finite extension, which depends on that supposition. But what need is there to insist on the particular sciences? Is not that opposition to all science whatsoever, that frenzy of the ancient and modern *skeptics,* built on the same foundation? Or can you produce so much as one argument against the reality of corporeal things, or in behalf of that avowed utter ignorance of their natures, which does not suppose their reality to consist in an external absolute existence? Upon this supposition indeed, the objections from the change of colors in a pigeon's neck, or the appearances of a broken oar in the water, must be allowed to have weight. But those and the like objections vanish, if we do not maintain the being of absolute external originals, but place the reality of things in ideas, fleeting indeed, and changeable; however not changed at random, but according to the fixed order of nature. For herein consists that constancy and truth of things, which secures all the concerns of life, and distinguishes that which is *real* from the irregular visions of the fancy.

    Hyl.   I agree to all you have now said, and must own that nothing can incline me to embrace your opinion, more than the advantages I see it is attended with. I am by nature lazy; and this would be a mighty abridgment in knowledge. What doubts, what hypotheses, what labyrinths of amusement, what fields of disputation, what an ocean of false learning, may be avoided by that single notion of *immaterialism?*

    Phil.   After all, is there anything farther remaining to be done? You may remember you promised to embrace that opinion, which upon examination should appear most agreeable to common sense, and remote from *skepticism.* This by your own confession is that which denies matter, or the absolute existence of corporeal things. Nor is this all; the same notion has been proved several ways, viewed in different lights, pursued in its consequences, and all objections against it cleared. Can there be a greater evidence of its truth? Or is it possible it should have all the marks of a true opinion, and yet be false?

Hyl.   I own myself entirely satisfied for the present in all respects. But what security can I have that I shall still continue the same full assent to your opinion, and that no unthought-of objection or difficulty will occur hereafter?

Phil.   Pray, Hylas, do you in other cases, when a point is once evidently proved, withhold your assent on account of objections or difficulties it may be liable to? Are the difficulties that attend the doctrine of incommensurable quantities, of the angle of contact, of the asymptotes to curves, or the like, sufficient to make you hold out against mathematical demonstration? Or will you disbelieve the providence of God, because there may be some particular things which you know not how to reconcile with it? If there are difficulties attending immaterialism, there are at the same time direct and evident proofs for it. But for the existence of matter, there is not one proof, and far more numerous and insurmountable objections lie against it. But where are those mighty difficulties you insist on? Alas! You know not where or what they are; something which may possibly occur hereafter. If this be a sufficient pretence for withholding your full assent, you should never yield it to any proposition, how free soever from exceptions, how clearly and solidly soever demonstrated.

Hyl.   You have satisfied me, Philonous.

Phil.   But to arm you against all future objections, do but consider, that which bears equally hard on two contradictory opinions, can be a proof against neither. Whenever therefore any difficulty occurs try if you can find a solution for it on the hypothesis of the *materialists*. Be not deceived by words; but sound your own thoughts. And in case you cannot conceive it easier by the help of *materialism*, it is plain it can be no objection against *immaterialism*. Had you proceeded all along by this rule, you would probably have spared yourself abundance of trouble in objecting; since of all your difficulties I challenge you to show one that is explained by matter; nay, which is not more unintelligible with than without that supposition, and consequently makes rather *against* than *for* it. You should consider, in each particular, whether the difficulty arises from the *nonexistence of matter*. If it does not, you might as well argue from the infinite divisibility of extension against the divine prescience, as from such a difficulty against *immaterialism*. And yet upon recollection I believe you will find this to have been often, if not always the case. You should likewise take heed not to argue on a *petitio principii*. One is apt to say, the unknown substances ought to be esteemed real things, rather than the ideas in our minds: and who can tell but the unthinking external substance may concur as a cause or instrument in the production of our ideas? But is not this proceeding on a supposition that there are such external substances? And to suppose this, is it not begging the question? But above all things you should beware of imposing on yourself by that vulgar sophism, which is called *ignoratio elenchi*. You talked often as if you thought I maintained the non-existence of sensible things: whereas in truth no one can be more thoroughly assured of their existence than I am: and it is you who doubt; I should have said, positively deny it. Everything that is seen, felt, heard, or any way perceived by the senses, is on the principles I embrace, a real being, but not on yours. Remember, the matter you contend for is an unknown somewhat (if indeed it may be termed *somewhat*) which is quite stripped of all sensible qualities, and can neither be perceived by sense, nor apprehended by the mind. Remember, I say, that it is not any object which is hard or soft, hot or cold, blue or white, round or square, &c. For all these things I affirm do exist. Though indeed I deny they have an existence distinct from being perceived; or that they exist out of all minds whatsoever. Think on these points; let them be attentively considered and still kept in view. Otherwise you will not comprehend the state of the question; without which your objections will always be wide of the mark, and instead of mine, may possibly be directed (as more than once they have been) against your own notions.

  Hyl. I must needs own, Philonous, nothing seems to have kept me from agreeing with you more than this same *mistaking the question*. In denying matter, at first glimpse I am tempted to imagine you deny the things we see and feel; but upon reflection find there is no ground for it. What think you therefore of retaining the name *matter*, and applying it to sensible things? This may be done without any change in your sentiments: and believe me it would be a means of reconciling them to some persons, who may be more shocked at an innovation in words than in opinion.

  Phil. With all my heart: retain the word *matter*, and apply it to the objects of sense, if you please, provided you do not attribute to them any subsistence distinct from their being perceived. I shall never quarrel with you for an expression. *Matter*, or *material substance*, are terms introduced by philosophers; and as used by them, imply a sort of independency, or a subsistence distinct from being perceived by a mind: but are never used by common people; or if ever, it is to signify the immediate objects of sense. One would think therefore, so long as the names of all particular things, with the terms *sensible, substance, body, stuff,* and the like, are retained, the word *matter* should be never missed in common talk. And in philosophical discourses it seems the best way to leave it quite out; since there is not perhaps any one thing that has more favored and strengthened the depraved bent of the mind toward atheism, than the use of that general confused term.

 Hyl. Well but, Philonous, since I am content to give up the notion of an unthinking substance exterior to the mind, I think you ought not to deny me the privilege of using the word *matter* as I please, and annexing it to a collection of sensible qualities subsisting only in the mind. I freely own there is no other substance, in a strict sense, than *spirit.* But I have been so long accustomed to the term *matter,* that I know not how to part with it. To say, there is no *matter* in the world, is still shocking to me. Whereas to say, there is no *matter,* if by that term be meant an unthinking substance existing without the mind: but if by *matter* is meant some sensible thing, whose existence consists in being perceived, then there is *matter:* this distinction gives it quite another turn: and men will come into your notions with small difficulty, when they are proposed in that manner. For after all, the controversy about *matter* in the strict acceptation of it, lies altogether between you and the philosophers; whose principles, I acknowledge, are not near so natural, or so agreeable to the common sense of mankind, and Holy Scripture, as yours. There is nothing we either desire or shun, but as it makes, or is apprehended to make, some part of our happiness or misery. But what has happiness or misery, joy or grief, pleasure or pain, to do with absolute existence, or with unknown entities, abstracted from all relation to us? It is evident, things regard us only as they are pleasing or displeasing: and they can please or displease, only so far forth as they are perceived. Farther therefore we are not concerned; and thus far you leave things as you found them. Yet still there is something new in this doctrine. It is plain, I do not now think with the philosophers, nor yet altogether with the vulgar. I would know how the case stands in that respect: precisely, what you have added to, or altered in my former notions.

 Phil. I do not pretend to be a setter-up of *new notions.* My endeavors tend only to unite, and place in a clearer light, that truth which was before shared between the vulgar and the philosophers: the former being of opinion, that *those things they immediately perceive are the real things;* and the latter, that *the things immediately perceived, are ideas which exist only in the mind.* Which two notions put together, do in effect constitute the substance of what I advance.

Hyl.   I have been a long time distrusting my sense; methought I saw things by a dim light, and through false glasses. Now the glasses are removed, and a new light breaks in upon my understanding. I am clearly convinced that I see things in their native forms; and am no longer in pain about their unknown natures or absolute existence. This is the state I find myself in at present: though indeed the course that brought me to it, I do not yet thoroughly comprehend. You set out upon the same principles that Academics, Cartesians, and the like sects, usually do; and for a long time it looked as if you were advancing their philosophical *skepticism;* but in the end your conclusions are directly opposite to theirs.

Phil.   You see, Hylas, the water of yonder fountain, how it is forced upwards, in a round column, to a certain height; at which it breaks and falls back into the basin from whence it rose: its ascent as well as descent, proceeding from the same uniform law or principle of *gravitation.* Just so, the same principles which at first view lead to *skepticism,* pursued to a certain point, bring men back to common sense.

Finis